CW00294477

family circle®

delicious Vegetarian FOOD

The Family Circle® Promise of Success

Welcome to the world of Confident Cooking, created for you in the Australian **Family Circle®** **Test Kitchen,** where recipes are double-tested by our team of home economists to achieve a high standard of success—and delicious results every time.

MURDOCH BOOKS®

Sydney • London • Vancouver • New York

CONTE

Corn and polenta pancakes with tomato salsa, page 18.

Vegetable shapes with crème fraîche and fried leek, page 35.

Vegetable and polenta pie, page 82.

Udon noodle stir-fry, page 58.

Vegetable tart with salsa verde, page 72.

Tomato, haloumi and spinach salad, page 29.

The Publisher thanks the following for their assistance: Chief Australia, Breville Holdings Pty Ltd, Kambrook, Sheldon & Hammond, Southcorp Appliances, Bertoli Olive Oil and Pillivuyt.
Front cover: Spinach and ricotta gnocchi (page 99) and Ratatouille tarte tartin (page 96).
Inside front cover: Vegetable casserole with herb dumplings (page 85).
Back cover: Felafel with tomato salsa (page 33).

All recipes are double-tested by our team of home economists. When we test our recipes, we rate them for ease of preparation. The following cookery ratings are on the recipes in this book, making them easy to use and understand.

A single Cooking with Confidence symbol indicates a recipe that is simple and generally quick to make—perfect for beginners.

Two symbols indicate the need for just a little more care and a little more time.

Three symbols indicate special dishes that need more investment in time, care and patience—but the results are worth it.

VEGAN
The vegan symbol indicates that all of the ingredients are of plant origin. For the purposes of this book, we have assumed that vegans cannot eat honey, but can eat yeast.

> **IMPORTANT**
> Those who might be at risk from the effects of salmonella food poisoning (the elderly, pregnant women, young children and those suffering from immune deficiency diseases) should consult their GP with any concerns about eating raw eggs.

Vegetable and tofu kebabs, page 108.

Spicy vegetable stew with dhal, page 74.

Vegetarian Glossary

Black sesame seeds: In their raw state, they have an earthy taste. If toasting, they need to be covered as they tend to pop.

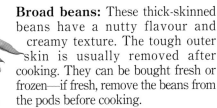

Broad beans: These thick-skinned beans have a nutty flavour and creamy texture. The tough outer skin is usually removed after cooking. They can be bought fresh or frozen—if fresh, remove the beans from the pods before cooking.

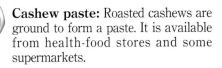

Cashew paste: Roasted cashews are ground to form a paste. It is available from health-food stores and some supermarkets.

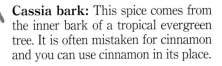

Cassia bark: This spice comes from the inner bark of a tropical evergreen tree. It is often mistaken for cinnamon and you can use cinnamon in its place.

Chilli jam: This sweet and sour jam is sold in jars at Asian food stores. Each brand varies in spiciness. For vegetarian cooking, make sure you read the label and choose one that doesn't contain shrimp paste.

Chinese dried mushrooms: Distinctly flavoured, this mixture of mushrooms needs to be soaked in boiling water for 10–15 minutes before use. Store them in a sealed container in a cool place.

Choy sum: This popular Chinese leaf vegetable has slightly bitter stems that are eaten more commonly than the leaves. Also known as flowering white cabbage.

Coconut cream and milk: Both are extracted from the grated flesh of mature coconuts. The cream is a richer first pressing and the milk the second or third pressing. When a recipe uses cream, don't shake the can; use the thick cream on top.

Couscous: This cereal is processed from semolina and coated with wheat flour. Instant couscous cooks in 5 minutes in boiling water.

Dried rice vermicelli: After soaking, these thin, translucent rice sticks develop a slippery texture and absorb the flavours of other food.

Ghee: A clarified unsalted butter used in Indian cooking. It has a higher burning point than other oils and fats.

Gow gee wrappers: These round wrappers are made from a wheat flour and water dough. They are usually used for steaming.

Haloumi cheese: A soft semi-hard cheese with a salty flavour made from sheep's or goat's milk.

Haricot beans: These small, white, oval beans have a bland flavour that absorbs other flavours well. Choose smooth-skinned beans with a creamy white colour.

Japanese soy sauce: This is much lighter and sweeter than Chinese soy sauce. It is naturally brewed, so refrigerate after opening.

Kaffir lime leaves: Highly fragrant, the leaves from the kaffir lime tree are used in curries, salads and soups. The leaves can be frozen. Dried leaves need to be soaked in boiling water.

Kecap manis: Widely used in Indonesian and Malaysian cooking, this is a thick sweet soy sauce. If it's not available, use soy sauce sweetened with a little soft brown sugar.

Kefalotyri cheese: A very hard, scalded cured sheep's or goat's milk cheese with a milder flavour than Parmesan. Buy at delicatessens.

Lentils: Packed with vitamins, there are many sizes, varieties and colours. Red, green and brown are the most common types. Green and brown lentils are often mixed together and can be substituted for each other. There's no need to soak lentils before cooking. They go mushy if cooked for too long.

Mirin: A sweet rice wine with a low alcohol content, mirin is used extensively in Japanese cooking.

Miso: Fermented tofu and grains left to mature and gradually darken in colour. **Shiro miso** is a very light-coloured, almost sweet miso suitable for salad dressings.

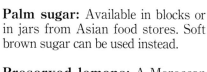

Nori sheets: The most common form of dried seaweed. It comes plain or roasted (for a more palatable flavour). The paper-thin sheets are usually used as a wrapper for sushi.

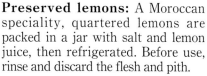

Palm sugar: Available in blocks or in jars from Asian food stores. Soft brown sugar can be used instead.

Preserved lemons: A Moroccan speciality, quartered lemons are packed in a jar with salt and lemon juice, then refrigerated. Before use, rinse and discard the flesh and pith.

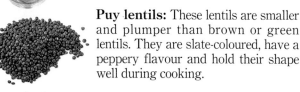

Puy lentils: These lentils are smaller and plumper than brown or green lentils. They are slate-coloured, have a peppery flavour and hold their shape well during cooking.

Rice-paper wrappers: With a distinctive basket-weave pattern, these square or round thin sheets are bought dried and will keep indefinitely, but be careful—they are very brittle. Before using, briefly soak them one at a time in warm water so they become pliable.

Rice vinegar: Made from vinegar and a natural rice extract. **Seasoned rice vinegar** is similar but has sugar and salt added.

Sake: A Japanese rice wine, sake is used as a drink and a cooking liquid.

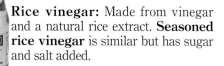

Soba noodles: Made from buckwheat flour, these noodles are usually available dried and sometimes fresh. They are eaten hot or cold.

Soya beans: Highly nutritious, these oval beans are the size of peas. The most common type is creamy yellow, but they are also red or black. Available fresh or dried, they need more cooking than other pulses.

Tahini: A thick paste made from ground white sesame seeds and sesame oil. It has a bitter flavour.

Tamari: Tamari is a naturally fermented dark soy sauce. Some varieties are wheat-free.

Tempeh: Similar to tofu, tempeh is made from fermented soya beans. Quite firm in texture, it is suitable for most types of cooking.

Tofu

SILKEN TOFU: A very soft tofu often used in soups. Take care when cooking with it or it will break up.

SILKEN FIRM TOFU: Slightly firmer than silken tofu, it holds its shape a little better. Use in soups.

FIRM TOFU: This soft tofu will hold its shape when cooking. It is suitable for stir-frying, pan-frying and baking.

HARD TOFU: Rubbery and firm, it won't break up during cooking. Use for stir-frying, pan-frying or as a base for patties.

TOFU TEMPEH: Tofu and tempeh are combined and pressed together. Use in the same way as firm tofu.

FRIED TOFU PUFFS: Tofu is aerated and then deep-fried. Use in stir-fries, curries and soups.

Vegetarian oyster sauce: This has a similar flavour to oyster sauce, but uses mushrooms as its flavour base.

Wakame: A curly-leaf brown algae with a mild vegetable taste and soft texture. Dried wakame can be used in salads or as a vegetable after boiling. Use sparingly—its volume increases by about 10 times. You can use kombu or other seaweeds if necessary.

Wasabi paste: From the edible root of a plant native to Japan. The skinned green root has a strong flavour like horseradish.

Won ton wrappers: Thin squares made from wheat flour and egg yolks.

Yellow split peas: A pea allowed to mature and dry on the vine. Normally dehusked and split. No soaking needed.

Items not available in the supermarket are available in specialist shops.

BREAKFASTS & BRUNCHES

POACHED EGGS WITH GARLIC YOGHURT DRESSING AND SPINACH

Preparation time: 10 minutes
Total cooking time: 15 minutes
Serves 4

1/2 cup (125 g) sheep's milk
    yoghurt
1 small clove garlic, crushed
1 tablespoon snipped fresh chives
300 g baby English spinach
    leaves, washed
30 g butter, chopped
herbed salt (see Note)
4 tomatoes, halved
1 tablespoon white vinegar
8 eggs
1 round loaf light rye bread,
    cut into eight thick slices

1 To make the dressing, mix together the yoghurt, garlic and chives.
2 Wash the spinach and place it in a large saucepan with a little water clinging to the leaves. Cook, covered, over low heat for 3–4 minutes, or until wilted. Add the butter. Season with herbed salt. Set aside and keep warm. Cook the tomatoes under a hot grill for 3–5 minutes.
3 Fill a frying pan three-quarters full with cold water and add the vinegar and some salt to stop the egg whites spreading. Bring to a gentle simmer. Gently break the eggs one by one into a small bowl, carefully slide each one into the water, then reduce the heat so that the water barely moves. Cook for 1–2 minutes, or until the eggs are just set. Remove with an egg flip. Drain.
4 Toast the bread. Top each slice of toast with spinach, an egg and some dressing. Serve with tomato halves.

NUTRITION PER SERVE
Protein 25 g; Fat 20 g; Carbohydrate 45 g; Dietary Fibre 7.5 g; Cholesterol 384 mg; 1895 kJ (453 cal)

COOK'S FILE

Note: Herbed salt is available at the supermarket.

Cook the spinach leaves until they are wilted, then stir in the butter.

Cook the eggs until they are just set, then remove with an egg flip.

MIXED BERRY COUSCOUS

Preparation time: 15 minutes
Total cooking time: 5 minutes
Serves 4

1 cup (185 g) instant couscous
2 cups (500 ml) apple and
    cranberry juice
1 cinnamon stick
2 teaspoons orange zest
250 g fresh raspberries
250 g fresh blueberries

250 g strawberries, halved
200 g Greek-style plain yoghurt
2 tablespoons golden syrup
fresh mint leaves, to garnish

1 Place the couscous in a bowl. Pour the apple and cranberry juice into a saucepan and add the cinnamon stick. Cover and bring to the boil, then remove from the heat and pour over the couscous. Cover the couscous with plastic wrap and leave for about 5 minutes, or until all the liquid has been absorbed. Remove the cinnamon stick from the bowl.

2 Separate the grains of couscous with a fork, then gently fold in the orange zest and most of the raspberries, blueberries and strawberries. Spoon the couscous mixture into four serving bowls and sprinkle with the remaining berries. Serve with a generous dollop of the yoghurt, then drizzle with the golden syrup. Garnish with fresh mint leaves and serve immediately.

NUTRITION PER SERVE
Protein 8.5 g; Fat 3 g; Carbohydrate 70 g;
Dietary Fibre 7 g; Cholesterol 8 mg;
1448 kJ (345 cal)

Pour the hot apple and cranberry juice over the couscous.

Separate the grains of couscous with a fork.

Gently fold in the raspberries, blueberries and strawberries.

PUFFED CORN CEREAL

Preparation time: 10 minutes
Total cooking time: 15 minutes
Serves 20 (Makes approx. 1.5 kg)

 VEGAN

85 g puffed corn
85 g puffed millet
2 x 200 g packets dried fruit
  and nut mix
180 g unprocessed natural bran

60 g flaked coconut
1/3 cup (60 g) pepitas
3/4 cup (185 ml) maple syrup
1 cup (70 g) processed bran
  cereal
2 x 200 g packets dried fruit
  salad mix, cut into small
  pieces

1 Preheat the oven to moderate 180°C (350°F/Gas 4). Spread out the corn, millet, fruit and nut mix, bran, coconut and pepitas in a large roasting tin.
2 Pour the maple syrup over the puffed corn mixture and stir until the dry ingredients are well coated.
3 Stir in the bran cereal and fruit salad mix and bake for 15 minutes, or until golden, turning the cereal several times during cooking. Cool completely.

NUTRITION PER SERVE
Protein 5 g; Fat 4 g; Carbohydrate 47 g; Dietary Fibre 9 g; Cholesterol 0 mg; 965 kJ (231 cal)

Using scissors, cut the dried fruit salad mixture into small pieces.

Spread out the puffed corn mixture in a large roasting tin.

Pour the maple syrup evenly over the dry ingredients.

RICOTTA PANCAKES WITH GOAT'S MILK YOGHURT AND PEARS

Preparation time: 15 minutes
Total cooking time: 50 minutes
Serves 4

1¹/₂ cups (185 g) plain flour
2 teaspoons baking powder
2 teaspoons ground ginger
2 tablespoons caster sugar
4 eggs, separated
350 g low-fat ricotta
1 pear, peeled, cored and grated
1¹/₄ cups (315 ml) milk
40 g butter
3 beurre bosc pears, unpeeled
40 g butter
1 tablespoon soft brown sugar
1 teaspoon ground cinnamon
200 g goat's milk yoghurt

1 Sift the flour, baking powder, ginger and sugar into a bowl and make a well in the centre. Pour the combined egg yolks, ricotta, grated pear and milk into the well and mix until smooth.
2 Beat the egg whites until soft peaks form, then fold into the mixture.
3 Heat a frying pan over medium heat and melt some of the butter. Pour ¹/₄ cup (60 ml) of the batter into the pan and swirl gently to create an even pancake. Cook for 1–1¹/₂ minutes, or until bubbles form on the surface, then turn and cook the other side for 1 minute, or until golden. Repeat with the remaining butter and mixture to make 11 more pancakes. Keep warm.
4 Cut the pears into thick slices lengthways. Melt the butter in a frying pan and add the sugar and cinnamon, then stir until the sugar dissolves. Add the pears and cook in batches, turning once, until golden and tender. Serve stacks of pancakes with the pears and yoghurt.

NUTRITION PER SERVE
Protein 26 g; Fat 41 g; Carbohydrate 85 g; Dietary Fibre 5.5 g; Cholesterol 266 mg; 3341 kJ (799 cal)

Stir the combined egg yolks, ricotta, grated pear and milk into the flour.

Cook the pancakes until bubbles form on the surface, then turn.

Cook the pears in batches in the buttery sauce, turning to coat in the mixture.

FRUIT SALAD IN VANILLA, GINGER AND LEMON GRASS SYRUP

Preparation time: 20 minutes +
  chilling time
Total cooking time: 15 minutes
Serves 4

 VEGAN

**500 g watermelon, cut into large
  cubes
260 g honeydew melon, cut into
  large cubes
1/2 small pineapple, cut into
  large pieces
1 mango, cut into 2 cm cubes
250 g strawberries, halved
1/4 cup (5 g) small mint sprigs**

Lemon grass syrup
**1/2 cup (125 ml) lime juice
1/4 cup (45 g) soft brown sugar
1 stem lemon grass, finely sliced
2 tablespoons grated fresh ginger
1 vanilla bean, split**

1 Place the fruit and mint in a bowl and mix gently.
2 To make the syrup, place the lime juice, sugar and 1/2 cup (125 ml) water in a small saucepan and stir over low heat until the sugar dissolves, then add the lemon grass, ginger and vanilla bean. Bring to the boil, reduce the heat and simmer for 10 minutes, or until reduced. Remove the vanilla bean, pour the syrup over the fruit and refrigerate until cold.

Remove the skin from the mango and cut the flesh into cubes.

NUTRITION PER SERVE
Protein 3.5 g; Fat 0.5 g; Carbohydrate 40 g; Dietary Fibre 6 g; Cholesterol 0 mg; 797 kJ (190 cal)

COOK'S FILE

Note: If you prefer your syrup without the lemon grass pieces but like the flavour, bruise the white part of the lemon grass with a rolling pin, place in the syrup, cook and remove along with the vanilla bean.

Simmer the lemon grass syrup until it is reduced and slightly thick.

BAKED RICOTTA WITH PRESERVED LEMON AND SEMI-DRIED TOMATOES

Preparation time: 15 minutes +
  10 minutes standing
Total cooking time: 30 minutes
Serves 8–10

2 kg wheel ricotta
olive oil spray
2 cloves garlic, crushed
1 preserved lemon, rinsed,
   pith and flesh removed,
   cut into thin strips
150 g semi-dried tomatoes,
   roughly chopped
1 cup (30 g) finely chopped
   fresh flat-leaf parsley
1 cup (50 g) chopped fresh
   coriander leaves
1/3 cup (80 ml) extra virgin
   olive oil
1/4 cup (60 ml) lemon juice

1 Preheat the oven to very hot 250°C (500°F/Gas 10). Place the ricotta on a baking tray lined with baking paper, spray lightly with the oil spray and bake for 20–30 minutes, or until golden brown. Stand for 10 minutes then, using egg flips, transfer to a large platter. (If possible, have someone help you move the ricotta.)
2 Meanwhile, place the garlic, preserved lemon, semi-dried tomato, parsley, coriander, oil and lemon juice in a bowl and mix together well.
3 Spoon the dressing over the baked ricotta, and serve with crusty bread. It is delicious hot or cold.

NUTRITION PER SERVE (10)
Protein 20 g; Fat 30 g; Carbohydrate 3 g; Dietary Fibre 0.5 g; Cholesterol 95 mg; 1542 kJ (368 cal)

Remove the flesh from the lemon and cut the rind into thin strips.

Mix all the dressing ingredients together in a bowl.

Spoon the dressing evenly over the baked ricotta.

FRIED TOMATOES WITH MARINATED HALOUMI

Preparation time: 15 minutes +
  overnight marinating
Total cooking time: 10 minutes
Serves 4

400 g haloumi cheese, cut into
  eight 1 cm slices
250 g cherry tomatoes, halved
250 g teardrop tomatoes, halved
1 clove garlic, crushed
2 tablespoons lemon juice
1 tablespoon balsamic vinegar
2 teaspoons fresh lemon thyme

1/4 cup (60 ml) extra virgin
  olive oil
2 tablespoons olive oil
1 small loaf good-quality
  wholegrain bread, cut
  into eight thick slices

1 Place the haloumi and tomatoes in a non-metallic dish. Whisk together the garlic, lemon juice, balsamic vinegar, thyme and extra virgin olive oil in a jug and pour over the haloumi and tomatoes. Cover and marinate for 3 hours or overnight. Drain well, reserving the marinade.
2 Heat the olive oil in a large frying pan. Add the haloumi and cook in batches over medium heat for 1 minute each side, or until golden brown. Transfer to a plate and keep warm. Add the tomatoes and cook over medium heat for 5 minutes, or until their skins begin to burst. Transfer to a plate and keep warm.
3 Toast the bread until it is golden brown. Serve the fried haloumi on top of the toasted bread, piled high with the tomatoes and drizzled with the reserved marinade. Serve immediately.

NUTRITION PER SERVE
Protein 30 g; Fat 40 g; Carbohydrate 34 g; Dietary Fibre 7 g; Cholesterol 53 mg; 2690 kJ (645 cal)

Pour the marinade over the haloumi and mixed tomatoes.

Cook the haloumi until golden brown on both sides.

Cook the tomatoes until their skins start to burst.

VEGETABLE, FETA AND PESTO PARCELS

Preparation time: 40 minutes
Total cooking time: 30 minutes
Serves 4

25 g butter
2 cloves garlic, crushed
155 g asparagus spears,
    trimmed and cut into
    2 cm pieces
1 carrot, cut into julienne strips
1 zucchini, cut into julienne
    strips
1 red capsicum, cut into julienne
    strips
6 spring onions, thinly sliced on
    the diagonal
80 g mild feta cheese, crumbled
8 sheets filo pastry
60 g butter, melted
1/3 cup (80 g) good-quality
    ready-made pesto
2 teaspoons sesame seeds

1 Preheat the oven to moderately hot 200°C (400°F/Gas 6). Heat the butter in a large frying pan, then add the garlic and vegetables. Cook over medium heat for 3–4 minutes, or until just tender. Cool completely and fold in the feta. Divide the mixture into four equal portions.

2 Work with four sheets of pastry at a time, keeping the rest covered with a damp tea towel. Brush each sheet with melted butter and lay them on top of one another. Cut in half widthways and spread 1 tablespoon of the pesto in the centre of each half, leaving a 2 cm border lengthways. Place one portion of the vegetable feta mixture on top of the pesto. Repeat the process with the remaining pastry, pesto and filling.

3 Brush the edges of filo with a little butter, tuck in the sides and fold over the ends to make four parcels. Place on a greased baking tray, seam-side-down, brush with the remaining butter and sprinkle with sesame seeds. Bake for 20–25 minutes, or until golden. Cut in half diagonally and serve hot with tomato chutney.

NUTRITION PER SERVE
Protein 28 g; Fat 16 g; Carbohydrate 126 g; Dietary Fibre 6 g; Cholesterol 30 mg; 3205 kJ (766 cal)

Cut the carrot and zucchini into julienne strips (the size and shape of matchsticks).

Cook the garlic and vegetables over medium heat until just tender.

Cover the pesto with one portion of the vegetable feta mixture.

Tuck in the sides and roll up the parcel until it sits on the unsecured end.

Quarter the capsicums, then remove the seeds and membranes.

Chargrill the eggplant, sweet potato and zucchini in batches until well browned.

Remove the soft bread from inside the loaf, leaving a 1 cm shell.

Layer the sweet potato and eggplant inside the loaf over the other ingredients.

MEDITERRANEAN LAYERED COB

Preparation time: 45 minutes +
  30 minutes standing + overnight
  refrigeration
Total cooking time: 30 minutes
Serves 6

2 eggplants
500 g orange sweet potato
2 large red capsicums
4 zucchini, cut into 1 cm slices
  lengthways
1/3 cup (80 ml) olive oil
23 cm round cob loaf
165 g good-quality ready-made
  pesto
200 g ricotta
1/3 cup (35 g) grated Parmesan

1 Cut the eggplants into 1 cm slices lengthways and put in a colander. Sprinkle with salt and leave for 30 minutes, then rinse well and pat dry with paper towels.

2 Cut the sweet potato into 5 mm slices. Quarter the capsicums and remove the seeds and membranes. Cook under a hot grill, skin-side-up, until the skins have blistered and blackened. Cool in a plastic bag, then peel. Brush the eggplant, sweet potato and zucchini with oil and chargrill or grill in batches until well browned.
3 Cut the lid from the top of the loaf. Remove the soft bread from inside, leaving a 1 cm shell. Brush the inside of the loaf and lid with the pesto. Layer the zucchini and capsicum inside the loaf, then spread with the combined ricotta and Parmesan. Layer the sweet potato and eggplant, lightly pressing down. Replace the lid.
4 Cover the loaf with plastic wrap and place on a baking tray. Put a tray on top of the loaf and weigh down with food cans. Refrigerate overnight.
5 Preheat the oven to very hot 250°C (500°F/Gas 10). Remove the plastic wrap, return the loaf to the baking tray and bake for about 10 minutes, or until crispy. Cut into wedges to serve.

NUTRITION PER SERVE
Protein 15 g; Fat 23 g; Carbohydrate 44 g; Dietary Fibre 7 g; Cholesterol 22 mg; 1870 kJ (447 cal)

Protein

Protein provides the basic structure for the human body—it is the main source of building material for our cells, tissues, muscles, nails, hair, skin, bones, blood and internal organs. We need protein to make and repair cells and tissues, and to create hormones, enzymes, antibodies and other immune-system molecules. It is also needed for the regulation of the body's internal environment, including acid and alkaline balance, water balance, and the proper elimination of wastes.

AND WHAT IS IT?

Protein is made up of small compounds known as amino acids, which are arranged in chains of varying combinations. There are approximately 22 amino acids, most of which are termed 'non-essential' as they can be made in the body.

But not all amino acids can be manufactured in the body—some must be derived from the diet, and these are termed the 'essential' amino acids. There are eight essential amino acids for adults—isoleucine, leucine, lysine, phenylalanine, methionine, threonine, tryptophan, valine—and an extra one, histidine, for infants.

Sources of these essential amino acids are animal products: meat, poultry, fish and dairy foods. There are also good vegetarian and vegan sources of protein: nuts and legumes (beans, peas, lentils, soya beans and products such as soy flour, soy milk, tofu and tempeh), but they don't have all the essential amino acids in the one food source like animal proteins do.

BEST LEGUMES FOR PROTEIN
Black beans
Black-eyed beans
Broad beans
Chickpeas
Kidney beans
Lentils
Mung beans
Navy beans
Peas
Soya beans

Plant proteins do have an advantage over animal proteins, as they contain fibre and carbohydrates, which makes them easy to digest as well as being high in vitamins and minerals and low in saturated fats and kilojoules.

IS PROTEIN COMBINING NECESSARY?

In the past it was thought that because the vegetarian sources of protein don't have all the essential amino acids, it was necessary to carefully combine them with other foods, such as wholegrains, to provide all the essential amino acids in their correct proportions.

However, recent research suggests that as long as there is a healthy mix of legumes, nuts, seeds, wholegrains and vegetables in the diet, the body will obtain enough protein for its needs. So, once again, the basic message is to have a balanced diet.

DAILY INTAKE

Our daily requirement of protein is approximately 12–20% of our total kilojoule intake, varying according to an individual's size, weight, levels of stress and activity, and health. Extra protein is needed during periods of growth: childhood, adolescence, pregnancy and lactation.

PROTEIN DEFICIENCY

Insufficient protein in the diet may result in such symptoms as anaemia, lethargy, muscle weakness and wasting, dry and dull hair, dry skin, poor wound healing, weak nails, outbursts of temper, decreased immunity to infection, bloating, digestive complaints and, in severe cases, amenorrhoea. Children with protein deficiency may not reach their full growth potential, while extreme cases of protein deficiency in children will result in the often fatal disease, kwashiorkor. However, Western vegetarians have very little chance of suffering from a protein deficiency.

PROTEIN IN EXCESS

In fact, in most Western diets, there is a much greater chance of consuming an excess of protein than there is of not consuming enough. Excess protein consumption can result in fluid imbalance, with symptoms such as diarrhoea, tissue swelling and frequent urination, which can lead to dehydration. It may also set up highly acidic conditions, which can lead to strong body odour, allergies, arthritis and gout. The extra burden on the digestive system may eventually cause liver and kidney damage.

SAMPLE MEAL IDEAS
BREAKFAST
- Muesli with soy milk (top with ground nuts/seeds and banana)
- Porridge with soy milk
- Baked beans on wholemeal toast
- Boiled egg with wholemeal toast
- Nut butter (e.g. almond, Brazil, cashew or peanut) on toast

LUNCH
- Lentil/bean/pea curry with rice
- Pumpkin and red lentil soup (page 67)
- Beetroot hummus (page 47) and salad in wholemeal pita bread
- Felafel with tomato salsa (page 33)
- Bean nachos (page 32) with avocado
- Miso soup with tofu, rice and vegetables
- Soya bean/tofu burger

DINNER
- Dahl and rice
- Tofu with rice and vegetables
- Mushroom risotto (page 98)
- Vegetable and tofu kebabs (page 108) with tomato sauce
- Mushroom nut roast with tomato sauce (page 70)

SNACKS
- Seeds (e.g. sesame or sunflower)
- Tamari nut mix (page 36)
- Tahini/hummus on wholewheat/rye/rice crackers

EXCELLENT PROTEIN SOURCE

Eggs, Cheddar, tempeh, lentils, ricotta (and other cheeses), sesame seeds, split green peas, peanuts, kidney beans, tofu.

VERY GOOD PROTEIN SOURCE

Bagels, English spinach, barley, bulgur, sunflower seeds, silver beet, chickpeas, cashew nuts, lima beans, cottage cheese, peas.

GOOD PROTEIN SOURCE

Bread, milk, fruit, vegetables, rice (brown and white), pasta, yoghurt.

CORN AND POLENTA PANCAKES WITH TOMATO SALSA

Preparation time: 15 minutes
Total cooking time: 10 minutes
Serves 4

Tomato salsa
2 ripe tomatoes
1 cup (150 g) frozen broad beans
2 tablespoons chopped fresh basil
1 small Lebanese cucumber, diced
2 small cloves garlic, crushed
1¹/2 tablespoons balsamic vinegar
1 tablespoon extra virgin olive oil

Corn and polenta pancakes
³/4 cup (90 g) self-raising flour
³/4 cup (110 g) fine polenta
1 cup (250 ml) milk
310 g can corn kernels, drained
olive oil, for pan-frying

1 Score a cross in the base of each tomato, then place in a bowl of boiling water for 30 seconds. Plunge into cold water and peel the skin away from the cross. Dice. Pour boiling water over the broad beans and leave for 2–3 minutes. Drain and rinse under cold water. Remove the skins. Put the beans in a bowl, add the tomato, basil, cucumber, garlic, vinegar and extra virgin olive oil and stir well.

2 To make the pancakes, sift the flour into a bowl and stir in the polenta. Add the milk and corn and stir until just combined, adding more milk if the mixture is too dry. Season.

3 Heat the oil in a large frying pan and spoon half the mixture into the frying pan, making four 9 cm pancakes. Cook for 2 minutes each side, or until golden and cooked through. Repeat with the remaining mixture, adding more oil if necessary. Drain on paper towels. Serve with the salsa.

NUTRITION PER SERVE
Protein 11 g; Fat 18.5 g; Carbohydrate 56 g; Dietary Fibre 8.5 g; Cholesterol 8.5 mg; 1809 kJ (432 cal)

After blanching, peel the skin off the broad beans.

Stir the milk and corn kernels into the flour and polenta mixture.

Cook the pancakes for 2 minutes each side, or until golden brown.

CARROT TIMBALES WITH CREAMY SAFFRON AND LEEK SAUCE

Preparation time: 25 minutes
Total cooking time: 1 hour
Serves 6

60 g butter
2 leeks, sliced
2 cloves garlic, crushed
1 kg carrots, sliced
1¹/2 cups (375 ml) vegetable
    stock
1¹/2 tablespoons finely chopped
    fresh sage
¹/4 cup (60 ml) cream
4 eggs, lightly beaten

Creamy saffron and leek sauce
40 g butter
1 small leek, finely sliced
1 large clove garlic, crushed
¹/4 cup (60 ml) white wine
pinch saffron threads
¹/3 cup (90 g) crème fraîche

1 Preheat the oven to warm 170°C (325°F/Gas 3). Lightly grease six ³/4 cup (185 ml) timbale moulds. Heat the butter in a saucepan over medium heat, add the leek and cook for 3–4 minutes, or until soft. Add the garlic and carrot and cook for a further 2–3 minutes. Pour in the stock and 2 cups (500 ml) water, bring to the boil, then reduce the heat and simmer, covered, for 5 minutes, or until the carrot is tender. Strain, reserving ³/4 cup (185 ml) of the liquid.
2 Blend the carrot mixture, ¹/2 cup (125 ml) of the reserved liquid and the sage in a food processor or blender until smooth. Cool the mixture slightly and stir in the cream and egg.

Season and pour into the prepared moulds. Place the moulds in a roasting tin filled with enough hot water to come halfway up their sides. Bake for 30–40 minutes, or until just set.
3 Meanwhile, to make the sauce, melt the butter in a saucepan and cook the leek over medium heat for 3–4 minutes without browning. Add the garlic and cook for 30 seconds. Add the wine,

remaining reserved liquid and saffron and bring to the boil. Reduce the heat and simmer for 5 minutes, or until reduced. Stir in the crème fraîche.
4 Invert the timbales onto serving plates and serve with the sauce.

NUTRITION PER SERVE
Protein 7 g; Fat 25 g; Carbohydrate 11 g; Dietary Fibre 6 g; Cholesterol 187 mg; 1258 kJ (300 cal)

Pour the mixture into the prepared moulds and place in a roasting tin.

Cook the leek, garlic, wine, reserved liquid and saffron on low heat until reduced.

Gently invert the carrot timbales onto serving plates.

MIXED MUSHROOMS IN BRIOCHE

Preparation time: 15 minutes
Total cooking time: 20 minutes
Serves 6

750 g mixed mushrooms
(Swiss brown, shiitake,
button, field, oyster)
75 g butter
4 spring onions, chopped
2 cloves garlic, crushed
1/2 cup (125 ml) dry white wine
300 ml cream
2 tablespoons chopped fresh
thyme
6 small brioche

1 Preheat the oven to moderate 180°C (350°F/Gas 4). Wipe the mushrooms with a clean damp cloth to remove any dirt. Cut the larger mushrooms into thick slices but leave the smaller ones whole.

2 Heat the butter in a large frying pan over medium heat. Add the spring onion and garlic and cook for 2 minutes. Increase the heat, add the mushrooms and cook, stirring frequently, for 5 minutes, or until the mushrooms are soft and all the liquid has evaporated. Pour in the wine and boil for 2 minutes to reduce slightly.

3 Stir in the cream and boil for a further 5 minutes to reduce and slightly thicken the sauce. Season to taste with salt and cracked black pepper. Stir in the thyme and set aside for 5 minutes.

4 Slice the top off the brioche and, using your fingers, pull out a quarter of the bread. Place the brioche and their tops on a baking tray and warm in the oven for 5 minutes.

5 Place each brioche onto individual serving plates. Spoon the mushroom sauce into each brioche, allowing it to spill over one side. Replace the top and serve warm.

NUTRITION PER SERVE
Protein 7.5 g; Fat 33 g; Carbohydrate 15 g; Dietary Fibre 4 g; Cholesterol 100 mg; 1587 kJ (380 cal)

C O O K ' S   F I L E

Note: Brioche are available from patisseries. You can use bread rolls instead, but the flavour isn't as good.

Cut the large mushrooms into thick slices, but leave the smaller ones whole.

Cook the mushrooms, stirring frequently, until they are soft.

Add the cream and cook until the sauce thickens slightly.

Pull a quarter of the bread out of the centre of the brioche.

WARM ASPARAGUS AND EGG SALAD WITH HOLLANDAISE

Preparation time: 5 minutes
Total cooking time: 15 minutes
Serves 4

Hollandaise
175 g butter
4 egg yolks
1 tablespoon lemon juice

4 eggs, at room temperature
310 g asparagus spears, trimmed
Parmesan shavings, to serve

1 To make the hollandaise, melt the butter in a small saucepan and skim off any froth. Remove from the heat and cool. Mix the egg yolks and 2 tablespoons water in another small saucepan for 30 seconds, or until pale and foamy. Place the saucepan over very low heat and whisk for 2–3 minutes, or until thick and foamy—do not overheat or it will scramble. Remove from the heat. Gradually add the butter, whisking well after each addition (avoid using the whey at the bottom). Stir in the lemon juice and season. If the sauce is runny, return to the heat and whisk until thick—do not scramble.

2 Place the eggs in a saucepan half filled with water. Bring to the boil and cook for 6–7 minutes, stirring occasionally to centre the yolks. Drain and cover with cold water until they can be handled, then peel off the shell.
3 Plunge the asparagus into a large saucepan of boiling water and cook for 3 minutes, or until just tender. Drain and pat dry. Divide among four plates. Spoon on the hollandaise. Cut the eggs in half and arrange two halves on each plate and top with Parmesan.

NUTRITION PER SERVE
Protein 13 g; Fat 47 g; Carbohydrate 1.5 g; Dietary Fibre 1 g; Cholesterol 475 mg; 1995 kJ (477 cal)

Whisk the yolks over very low heat until thick, foamy and the whisk leaves a trail.

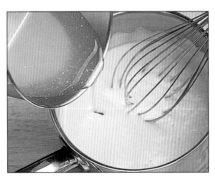

Gradually add the cooled butter, whisking well between each addition.

Cook the asparagus in a large saucepan of boiling water until just tender.

LUNCHES & LIGHT MEALS

FRESH BEETROOT AND GOAT'S CHEESE SALAD

Preparation time: 20 minutes
Total cooking time: 30 minutes
Serves 4

1 kg (4 bulbs with leaves) fresh
    beetroot
200 g green beans
1 tablespoon red wine vinegar
2 tablespoons extra virgin olive
    oil
1 clove garlic, crushed
1 tablespoon drained capers,
    coarsely chopped
100 g goat's cheese

1 Trim the leaves from the beetroot. Scrub the bulbs and wash the leaves well. Add the whole bulbs to a large saucepan of boiling water, reduce the heat and simmer, covered, for 30 minutes, or until tender when pierced with the point of a knife. (The cooking time may vary depending on the size of the bulbs.)

2 Meanwhile, bring a saucepan of water to the boil, add the beans and cook for 3 minutes, or until just tender. Remove with a slotted spoon and plunge into a bowl of cold water. Drain well. Add the beetroot leaves to the same saucepan of boiling water and cook for 3–5 minutes, or until the leaves and stems are tender. Drain, plunge into a bowl of cold water, then drain again well.

3 Drain and cool the beetroots, then peel the skins off and cut the bulbs into thin wedges.

4 To make the dressing, put the red wine vinegar, oil, garlic, capers, 1/2 teaspoon salt and 1/2 teaspoon pepper in a screw-top jar and shake.

5 To serve, divide the beans, beetroot leaves and bulbs among four serving plates. Crumble goat's cheese over the top and drizzle with the dressing.

NUTRITION PER SERVE
Protein 12 g; Fat 18 g; Carbohydrate 22 g; Dietary Fibre 9 g; Cholesterol 25 mg; 1256 kJ (300 cal)

Remove the skin from the beetroot, then cut into thin wedges.

Cook the beetroot leaves until the leaves and stems are tender.

INDIVIDUAL VEGETABLE TERRINES WITH A SPICY TOMATO SAUCE

Preparation time: 40 minutes
Total cooking time: 50 minutes
Serves 4

1/2 cup (125 ml) oil
2 zucchini, sliced on the diagonal
500 g eggplant, sliced
1 small fennel bulb, sliced
1 red onion, sliced
300 g ricotta
1/2 cup (50 g) grated Parmesan
1 tablespoon chopped fresh
    flat-leaf parsley
1 tablespoon chopped fresh
    chives
1 red capsicum, grilled, peeled
    and cut into large pieces
1 yellow capsicum, grilled, peeled
    and cut into large pieces

Spicy tomato sauce
1 tablespoon oil
1 onion, finely chopped
2 cloves garlic, crushed
1 red chilli, seeded and chopped
425 g can chopped tomatoes
2 tablespoons tomato paste

1 Heat 1 tablespoon of the oil in a large frying pan. Cook the vegetables in separate batches over high heat for 5 minutes, or until golden, adding the remaining oil as needed. Drain each vegetable separately on paper towels.
2 Preheat the oven to moderately hot 200°C (400°F/Gas 6). Place the cheeses and herbs in a small bowl and mix together well. Season to taste.
3 Lightly grease four 1 1/4 cup (315 ml) ramekins and line with baking paper. Using half the eggplant, put a layer in the base of each dish. Layer the zucchini, capsicum, cheese mixture, fennel and onion over the eggplant. Cover with the remaining eggplant and press down firmly. Bake for 10–15 minutes, or until hot. Leave for 5 minutes before turning out.
4 Meanwhile, to make the sauce, heat the oil in a saucepan and cook the onion and garlic for 2–3 minutes, or until soft. Add the chilli, tomato and tomato paste and simmer for 5 minutes, or until thick and pulpy. Purée in a food processor. Return to the saucepan and keep warm. Spoon over the terrines.

NUTRITION PER SERVE
Protein 18 g; Fat 48 g; Carbohydrate 16 g; Dietary Fibre 8.5 g; Cholesterol 48 mg; 2346 kJ (560 cal)

Cook the capsicums under a hot grill until blackened. Cool, peel, then cut into pieces.

Layer the fennel over the cheese mixture, then add a layer of onion.

Simmer the tomato sauce for 5 minutes, or until thick and pulpy.

ASPARAGUS AND MUSHROOM SALAD

Preparation time: 20 minutes
Total cooking time: 10 minutes
Serves 4

155 g asparagus spears
1 tablespoon wholegrain
   mustard
1/4 cup (60 ml) orange juice
2 tablespoons lemon juice
1 tablespoon lime juice
1 tablespoon orange zest
2 teaspoons lemon zest

2 teaspoons lime zest
2 cloves garlic, crushed
1/4 cup (90 g) honey
400 g button mushrooms, halved
150 g rocket
1 red capsicum, cut into strips

1 Trim the woody ends from the asparagus spears and cut in half on the diagonal. Place in a saucepan of boiling water and cook for 1 minute, or until just tender. Drain, plunge into cold water and set aside.
2 Place the mustard, citrus juice and zest, garlic and honey in a large saucepan and season with pepper.

Bring to the boil, then reduce the heat and add the mushrooms, tossing for 2 minutes. Cool.
3 Remove the mushrooms from the sauce with a slotted spoon. Return the sauce to the heat, bring to the boil, then reduce the heat and simmer for 3–5 minutes, or until reduced and syrupy. Cool slightly.
4 Toss the mushrooms, rocket leaves, capsicum and asparagus. Place on a plate and drizzle with the sauce.

NUTRITION PER SERVE
Protein 6 g; Fat 0 g; Carbohydrate 25 g; Dietary Fibre 5 g; Cholesterol 0 mg; 550 kJ (132 cal)

Use a zester to remove the zest of the orange, lemon and lime.

Toss the mushrooms in the mustard, juices, zest, garlic and honey.

Simmer the sauce until it is reduced and syrupy.

TOFU WITH CARROT AND GINGER SAUCE

Preparation time: 25 minutes +
  overnight refrigeration
Total cooking time: 30 minutes
Serves 6

  VEGAN

2 x 300 g packets firm tofu
1/2 cup (125 ml) orange juice
1 tablespoon soft brown sugar
1 tablespoon soy sauce
2 tablespoons chopped fresh
  coriander leaves
2 cloves garlic, crushed
1 teaspoon grated fresh ginger
2–3 tablespoons oil
1 kg baby bok choy, cut into
  quarters lengthways

Carrot and ginger sauce
300 g carrots, chopped
2 teaspoons grated fresh ginger
2/3 cup (170 ml) orange juice
1/2 cup (125 ml) vegetable stock

1 Drain the tofu, then slice each block into six lengthways. Place in a single layer in a flat non-metallic dish. Mix the juice, sugar, soy sauce, coriander, garlic and ginger in a jug, then pour over the tofu. Cover and refrigerate overnight, turning once.
2 Drain the tofu, reserving the marinade. Heat the oil in a large frying pan and cook the tofu in batches over high heat for 2–3 minutes each side, or until golden. Remove and keep warm. Bring the marinade to the boil in a saucepan, then reduce the

heat and simmer for 1 minute. Remove from the heat and keep warm.
3 Heat a wok, add the bok choy and 1 tablespoon water and cook, covered, over medium heat for 2–3 minutes, or until tender. Remove and keep warm.
4 Add all the sauce ingredients to a saucepan, bring to the boil, then reduce the heat and simmer, covered, for 5–6 minutes, or until the carrot is tender. Transfer to a food processor and blend until smooth.
5 To serve, divide the bok choy among six plates. Top with some sauce, then the tofu and drizzle on a little of the marinade before serving.

NUTRITION PER SERVE
Protein 14 g; Fat 14 g; Carbohydrate 14 g; Dietary Fibre 8.5 g; Cholesterol 0 mg; 1034 kJ (246 cal)

Lay the tofu slices in a flat dish and pour on the marinade.

Cook the tofu slices in batches until golden brown on both sides.

Blend the carrot mixture in a food processor until smooth.

ROASTED TOMATOES AND EGGPLANT WITH RED LENTIL PUREE

Preparation time: 20 minutes
Total cooking time: 1 hour 10 minutes
Serves 6

 VEGAN

¹/₄ cup (60 ml) extra virgin olive oil
1 tablespoon balsamic vinegar
700 g egg (Roma) tomatoes, halved lengthways
500 g eggplant, cut into 1.5 cm slices
150 g rocket
¹/₄ cup (40 g) pine nuts, toasted

Red lentil purée
2¹/₂ cups (625 ml) vegetable stock
200 g red lentils
1 teaspoon paprika
1 clove garlic, crushed

1 Preheat the oven to moderate 180°C (350°F/Gas 4). Line a large baking tray with foil and grease with oil. To make the balsamic vinaigrette, place the oil, vinegar, ¹/₄ teaspoon salt and ¹/₄ teaspoon cracked black pepper in a small bowl and whisk well.

2 Place the tomatoes, cut-side-up, and eggplant on the baking tray and brush with 1 tablespoon of the balsamic vinaigrette. Bake for 40 minutes. Transfer the eggplant to a plate and keep warm. Return the tomatoes to the oven and bake for 30 minutes, or until starting to brown on the edges. Transfer to a plate.

3 Meanwhile, to make the lentil purée, place the stock in a saucepan and bring to the boil. Add the lentils and paprika, return to the boil, then reduce the heat and simmer for 10 minutes, or until the lentils are tender. Add 1 tablespoon of the balsamic vinaigrette, then the garlic and continue stirring for 5 minutes, or until the lentils break up and form a thick purée. Season.

4 To serve, divide the red lentil purée among six serving plates. Top with the rocket leaves, then the eggplant and tomato. Drizzle with the remaining balsamic vinaigrette and sprinkle with pine nuts. Serve with crusty bread.

NUTRITION PER SERVE
Protein 11 g; Fat 15 g; Carbohydrate 16 g; Dietary Fibre 8.5 g; Cholesterol 0 mg; 1035 kJ (245 cal)

Place the oil, vinegar, salt and pepper in a small bowl and whisk.

Bake the tomatoes until they are shrivelled and just brown on the edges.

Cook the lentil mixture until the lentils break up and form a thick purée.

EGGPLANT, TOMATO AND GOAT'S CHEESE STACKS

Preparation time: 15 minutes
Total cooking time: 20 minutes
Serves 4

1/2 cup (125 ml) olive oil
2 large cloves garlic, crushed
2 small eggplants
2 ripe tomatoes
150 g goat's cheese
8 basil leaves
small rocket leaves, to garnish

Dressing
285 g jar sun-dried tomatoes,
    drained, reserving
    1 tablespoon oil
1 clove garlic, crushed
2 tablespoons white wine
    vinegar
2 tablespoons whole-egg
    mayonnaise

1 Place the oil and garlic in a bowl and mix together. Cut each eggplant into six 1 cm slices, then cut each tomato into four 1 cm slices. Using a sharp knife dipped in hot water, cut the cheese into eight 1 cm slices.
2 Brush both sides of the eggplant with half of the oil mixture. Heat a frying pan and cook the eggplant in batches over high heat for 3–4 minutes each side, or until golden. Remove and keep warm. Brush both sides of the tomato with the remaining oil mixture and cook for 1 minute each side, or until sealed and warmed through.
3 To make the dressing, blend the sun-dried tomatoes, reserved oil and the garlic in a food processor until smooth. Add the vinegar and process until combined. Transfer to a bowl and stir in the mayonnaise. Season.
4 To assemble, place an eggplant slice on each plate. Top with a slice of tomato, then a basil leaf and a slice of cheese. Repeat with the remaining ingredients to give two layers, then finish with a third piece of eggplant. Add a dollop of dressing and arrange the rocket around each stack. Serve immediately.

NUTRITION PER SERVE
Protein 12 g; Fat 35 g; Carbohydrate 7 g; Dietary Fibre 3.5 g; Cholesterol 43 mg; 1630 kJ (389 cal)

Cut the eggplant, tomato and cheese into 1 cm slices.

Cook the eggplant over high heat for 3–4 minutes each side, or until golden.

Cook the tomato slices on both sides until sealed and warmed through.

Stir the mayonnaise into the sun-dried tomato mixture.

TOMATO, HALOUMI AND SPINACH SALAD

Preparation time: 15 minutes +
  2 hours marinating
Total cooking time: 1 hour
Serves 4

200 g haloumi cheese
1/4 cup (60 ml) olive oil
2 cloves garlic, crushed
1 tablespoon chopped fresh
  oregano
1 tablespoon chopped fresh
  marjoram
8 egg (Roma) tomatoes, halved

1 small red onion, cut into eight
  wedges with base intact
1/4 cup (60 ml) olive oil, extra
2 tablespoons balsamic vinegar
150 g baby English spinach
  leaves

1 Cut the haloumi into 1 cm slices lengthways and place in a shallow dish. Mix the oil, garlic and herbs in a jug and pour over the haloumi. Marinate, covered, for 1–2 hours.

2 Preheat the oven to moderately hot 200°C (400°F/Gas 6). Place the tomato and onion in a single layer in a roasting tin, drizzle with 2 tablespoons of the extra olive oil and 1 tablespoon of the vinegar and sprinkle with salt and cracked black pepper. Bake for 50–60 minutes, or until golden.

3 Meanwhile, heat a non-stick frying pan over medium heat. Drain the haloumi and cook for 1 minute each side, or until golden brown.

4 Divide the spinach leaves among four serving plates and top with the tomato and onion. Whisk together the remaining olive oil and balsamic vinegar in a small bowl and drizzle over the salad. Top with the haloumi.

NUTRITION PER SERVE
Protein 14 g; Fat 27 g; Carbohydrate 6.5 g;
Dietary Fibre 4 g; Cholesterol 26 mg;
1333 kJ (320 cal)

Cut the onion into eight wedges, keeping the base intact.

Bake the tomatoes and onion in a roasting tin until golden.

Cook both sides of the drained haloumi in a frying pan until golden brown.

ASIAN GREENS WITH TERIYAKI TOFU DRESSING

Preparation time: 15 minutes
Total cooking time: 20 minutes
Serves 6

 VEGAN

650 g baby bok choy
500 g choy sum
440 g snake beans, topped and tailed
1/4 cup (60 ml) oil
1 onion, thinly sliced
1/3 cup (60 g) soft brown sugar
1/2 teaspoon ground chilli
2 tablespoons grated fresh ginger
1 cup (250 ml) teriyaki sauce
1 tablespoon sesame oil
600 g silken firm tofu, drained

1 Cut the the baby bok choy and choy sum widthways into thirds. Cut the snake beans into 10 cm lengths.
2 Heat a wok over high heat, add 1 tablespoon of the oil and swirl to coat the side. Cook the onion in batches for 3–5 minutes, or until crisp. Remove with a slotted spoon and drain on paper towels.
3 Heat 1 tablespoon of the oil in the wok, add half the greens and stir-fry for 2–3 minutes, or until wilted. Remove and keep warm. Repeat with the remaining oil and greens. Remove. Drain any liquid from the wok.
4 Add the combined sugar, chilli, ginger and teriyaki sauce to the wok and bring to the boil. Simmer for 1 minute. Add the sesame oil and tofu and simmer for 2 minutes, turning once—the tofu will break up. Divide the greens among serving plates, then top with the dressing. Sprinkle with the fried onion.

NUTRITION PER SERVE
Protein 19 g; Fat 11 g; Carbohydrate 20 g; Dietary Fibre 11 g; Cholesterol 1 mg; 1093 kJ (260 cal)

Cut the baby bok choy and choy sum widthways into thirds.

Cook the combined greens in two batches until the leaves are wilted.

Turn the tofu with an egg-flip halfway through cooking.

MISO TOFU STICKS WITH CUCUMBER AND WAKAME SALAD

Preparation time: 30 minutes +
  20 minutes standing
Total cooking time: 15 minutes
Serves 4

3 Lebanese cucumbers, thinly
  sliced into rounds
20 g dried wakame
500 g silken firm tofu, well
  drained
1/4 cup (60 ml) shiro miso
1 tablespoon mirin
1 tablespoon sugar
1 tablespoon rice vinegar
1 egg yolk
100 g bean sprouts, blanched
2 tablespoons sesame seeds,
  toasted

Dressing
1/4 cup (60 ml) rice vinegar
1/4 teaspoon soy sauce
1 1/2 tablespoons sugar
1 tablespoon mirin

1 Sprinkle the cucumber generously with salt and leave for 20 minutes, or until very soft, then rinse and drain. To rehydrate the wakame, place it in a colander in the sink and leave it under cold running water for 10 minutes, then drain well.
2 Place the tofu in a colander, weigh down with a plate and leave to drain.
3 Place the shiro miso, mirin, sugar, rice vinegar and 2 tablespoons water in a saucepan and stir over low heat for 1 minute, or until the sugar dissolves. Remove from the heat, then add the egg yolk and whisk until glossy. Cool slightly.

4 Cut the tofu into thick sticks and place on a non-stick baking tray. Brush the miso mixture over the tofu and cook under a hot grill for 6 minutes each side, or until light golden on both sides.
5 To make the dressing, place all the ingredients and 1/2 teaspoon salt in a bowl and whisk together well.

6 To assemble, place the cucumber in the centre of a plate, top with the sprouts and wakame, drizzle with the dressing, top with tofu and serve sprinkled with the sesame seeds.

NUTRITION PER SERVE
Protein 10 g; Fat 7 g; Carbohydrate 8 g; Dietary Fibre 2.5 g; Cholesterol 0 mg; 710 kJ (180 cal)

Once the cucumber is very soft, rinse the salt off under running water.

Place the wakame in a colander and leave it under cold running water.

Brush the miso mixture over the tofu sticks and grill under golden.

BEAN NACHOS

Preparation time: 20 minutes
Total cooking time: 10 minutes
Serves 4

4 large ripe tomatoes
2 ripe avocados, mashed
1 tablespoon lime juice
1 tablespoon sweet chilli sauce
1 tablespoon oil
2 small red onions, diced
1 small red chilli, chopped
2 teaspoons ground oregano
2 teaspoons ground cumin
1/4 teaspoon chilli powder

1 tablespoon tomato paste
1 cup (250 ml) white wine
2 x 440 g cans red kidney
  beans, rinsed and drained
3 tablespoons chopped fresh
  coriander leaves
200 g packet natural corn chips
2/3 cup (85 g) grated Cheddar
sour cream, to serve

1 Score a cross in the base of each tomato. Put them in a bowl of boiling water for 30 seconds, then plunge into cold water and peel the skin away from the cross. Cut in half and scoop out the seeds with a teaspoon. Chop.
2 Place the avocado, lime juice and

sweet chilli sauce in a bowl and mix.
3 Heat the oil in a large frying pan. Cook the onion, chilli, oregano, cumin and chilli powder over medium heat for 2 minutes. Add the tomato, tomato paste and wine and cook for 5 minutes, or until the liquid reduces. Add the beans and coriander.
4 Divide the corn chips into four. Top with the bean mixture and sprinkle with cheese. Cook under a hot grill until the cheese melts. Serve with the avocado mixture and sour cream.

NUTRITION PER SERVE
Protein 26 g; Fat 35 g; Carbohydrate 53 g; Dietary Fibre 20 g; Cholesterol 20 mg; 2845 kJ (680 cal)

Scoop out the seeds of the tomatoes and roughly chop the flesh.

Cook the onion, chilli, oregano and spices in a large frying pan.

Cook the mixture until the liquid is reduced and the tomato is soft.

FELAFEL WITH TOMATO SALSA

Preparation time: 40 minutes + 4 hours
  soaking + 30 minutes standing
Total cooking time: 20 minutes
Serves 8

 VEGAN

2 cups (440 g) dried chickpeas
1 small onion, finely chopped
2 cloves garlic, crushed
4 tablespoons chopped fresh
  flat-leaf parsley
2 tablespoons chopped fresh
  coriander leaves
2 teaspoons ground cumin
1/2 teaspoon baking powder
oil, for deep-frying

Tomato salsa
2 tomatoes
1/4 Lebanese cucumber, finely
  chopped
1/2 green capsicum, diced
2 tablespoons chopped fresh
  flat-leaf parsley
1 teaspoon sugar
2 teaspoons chilli sauce
1/2 teaspoon grated lemon rind
2 tablespoons lemon juice

1 Soak the chickpeas in 1 litre water for 4 hours or overnight. Drain. Place in a food processor and blend for 30 seconds, or until finely ground. Add the onion, garlic, parsley, coriander, cumin, baking powder and 1 tablespoon water, then process for 10 seconds, or until a rough paste. Leave, covered, for 30 minutes.

2 To make the salsa, score a cross in the base of each tomato. Put them in a bowl of boiling water for 30 seconds, then plunge into cold water and peel the skin away from the cross. Finely chop, then place in a bowl with all the other ingredients and mix well.

3 Using your hands, shape heaped tablespoons of the felafel mixture into even-sized balls. If there is any excess liquid, squeeze it out. Fill a large heavy-based saucepan one third full of oil and heat until a cube of bread dropped into the oil browns in 15 seconds. Lower the felafel balls into the oil and cook in batches of five for 3–4 minutes, or until well browned all over. Remove the felafel with a slotted spoon and drain on paper towels.

4 Serve the felafel hot or cold on a bed of the tomato salsa.

NUTRITION PER SERVE
Protein 10.5 g; Fat 8 g; Carbohydrate 22.5 g; Dietary Fibre 8 g; Cholesterol 0 mg; 855 kJ (204 cal)

Grind the drained chickpeas in a food processor until finely chopped.

Shape heaped tablespoons of the felafel mixture into even-sized balls.

Cook until well browned, then remove them with a slotted spoon and drain.

APPETISERS & ENTREES

VEGETABLE SHAPES WITH CRÈME FRAICHE AND FRIED LEEK

Preparation time: 25 minutes
Total cooking time: 45 minutes
Makes 35

2 (850 g in total) long thin
   orange sweet potatoes
5 beetroots
1/2 cup (125 g) crème fraîche
1 clove garlic, crushed
1/4 teaspoon grated lime rind
oil, for deep-frying
2 leeks, cut lengthways into
   very fine slices

1 Bring two large saucepans of water to the boil over high heat and place the sweet potatoes in one saucepan and the beetroots in the other. Boil, covered, for 30–40 minutes, or until tender, adding more boiling water if it starts to evaporate. Drain separately and set aside until cool enough to touch. Remove the skins from the beetroots. Trim the ends from the beetroots and sweet potatoes and cut both into 1 cm slices. Using a biscuit cutter, cut the thin slices into shapes.

Leave to drain on paper towels.
2 Place the crème fraîche, garlic and lime rind in a bowl and mix together well. Refrigerate until ready to use.
3 Fill a deep heavy-based saucepan one third full of oil and heat until a cube of bread dropped into the oil browns in 10 seconds. Cook the leek in four batches for 30 seconds, or until golden brown and crisp. Drain on crumpled paper towels and season with salt.
4 To assemble, place a teaspoon of the crème fraîche mixture on top of each vegetable shape and top with some fried leek.

NUTRITION PER VEGETABLE SHAPE
Protein 1 g; Fat 2 g; Carbohydrate 5.5 g;
Dietary Fibre 1 g; Cholesterol 2.5 mg;
180 kJ (43 cal)

COOK'S FILE

Hint: You can make the crème fraîche mixture and deep-fry the leek a day before and keep them in separate airtight containers. Refrigerate the crème fraîche mixture to allow the flavours to infuse. If the leek softens, place on a baking tray and crisp in a hot oven for 5 minutes. Assemble at the last minute to prevent the crème fraîche running.

Using a biscuit cutter, cut the beetroot and sweet potato into shapes.

Cook the leek in batches until golden brown and crisp.

TAMARI NUT MIX

Preparation time: 5 minutes +
  10 minutes standing
Total cooking time: 25 minutes
Serves 10–12 (Makes 4 cups)

 VEGAN

**250 g mixed nuts (almonds,
  Brazil nuts, peanuts,
  walnuts)**
125 g pepitas (see Note)
125 g sunflower seeds
125 g cashew nuts
125 g macadamia nuts
1/2 cup (125 ml) tamari

1 Preheat the oven to very slow 140°C (275°F/Gas 1). Lightly grease two large baking trays.
2 Place the mixed nuts, pepitas, sunflower seeds, cashew nuts and macadamia nuts in a large bowl. Pour the tamari over the nuts and seeds and toss together well, coating them evenly in the tamari. Leave for 10 minutes.
3 Spread the nut and seed mixture evenly over the prepared baking trays and bake for 20–25 minutes, or until dry roasted. Cool completely and store in an airtight container for up to 2 weeks. Serve as a snack.

NUTRITION PER SERVE (12)
Protein 11.5 g; Fat 36 g; Carbohydrate 4 g; Dietary Fibre 5 g; Cholesterol 0 mg; 1604 kJ (383 cal)

COOK'S FILE

Notes: Pepitas are peeled pumpkin seeds—they are available at most supermarkets and health-food stores.
  The nut mixture won't crisp to its full potential until it is cooled.
Storage: Once stored, the nut mixture may become soft. If it does, lay the nuts out flat on a baking tray and bake in a slow (150°C/300°F/ Gas 2) oven for 5–10 minutes.

Stir the tamari through the nuts, pepitas and sunflower seeds.

Spread the nut mixture evenly over two lightly greased baking trays.

Cook the nut mixture in the oven for 20–25 minutes, or until dry roasted.

ASSORTED VEGETABLE CHIPS

Preparation time: 20 minutes
Total cooking time: 15 minutes
Serves 6–8

 VEGAN

250 g orange sweet potato
250 g beetroot, peeled
250 g potato
oil, for deep-frying

1 Preheat the oven to moderate 180°C (350°F/Gas 4). Run a sharp vegetable peeler along the length of the sweet potato to create ribbons. Cut the beetroot into paper-thin slices using a sharp vegetable peeler or knife. Cut the potato into thin slices using a mandolin slicer or knife with a crinkle-cut blade.

2 Fill a deep heavy-based saucepan one third full of oil and heat until a cube of bread dropped into the oil browns in 10 seconds. Cook the vegetables in batches for about 30 seconds, or until golden and crispy. You may need to turn them with tongs or a long-handled metal spoon. Drain on crumpled paper towels and season with salt.

3 Place all the vegetable chips on a baking tray and keep warm in the oven while cooking the remaining vegetables. Serve with drinks.

NUTRITION PER SERVE (8)
Protein 2 g; Fat 5 g; Carbohydrate 12 g; Dietary Fibre 2 g; Cholesterol 0 mg; 413 kJ (99 cal)

COOK'S FILE

Note: These vegetables can be cut any way you prefer. If you don't have a mandolin or crinkle-cut knife at home, simply use a sharp knife to cut fine slices. The cooking time for the chips will remain the same.

Use a sharp vegetable peeler to peel thin strips of sweet potato.

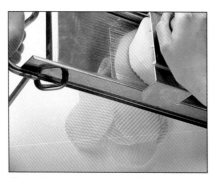

Cut the potato into slices using a mandolin slicer.

Deep-fry the vegetables in batches until they are golden and crispy.

EGGPLANT AND CORIANDER TOSTADAS

Preparation time: 20 minutes
Total cooking time: 30 minutes
Serves 4

 VEGAN

1 small eggplant, cut into cubes
1/2 red capsicum, cut into cubes
1/2 red onion, cut into thin
    wedges
2 tablespoons olive oil
1 large clove garlic, crushed
1 small loaf wood-fired bread,
    cut into twelve 1.5 cm slices
1 small ripe tomato, halved
2 tablespoons chopped fresh
    mint

2 tablespoons chopped fresh
    coriander roots, stems and
    leaves
50 g slivered almonds, toasted

1 Preheat the oven to very hot 240°C (475°F/Gas 9). Place the eggplant, capsicum, onion and oil in a large bowl and mix until the vegetables are well coated in the oil. Spread the vegetables in a single layer in a large roasting tin. Bake for 15 minutes, then turn and bake for a further 10 minutes, or until tender. Transfer to a bowl, add the garlic and season to taste with salt and pepper.
2 Place the bread on a baking tray and bake for 4 minutes, or until crisp. Rub the cut side of the tomato onto

one side of the bread slices, squeezing the tomato to extract as much liquid as possible, then finely chop the tomato flesh and add to the vegetables along with the mint and coriander.
3 Spoon the vegetable mixture onto the tomato side of the bread and sprinkle with the almonds. Serve immediately.

NUTRITION PER SERVE
Protein 10 g; Fat 18 g; Carbohydrate 34 g; Dietary Fibre 5 g; Cholesterol 0 mg; 1415 kJ (340 cal)

COOK'S FILE

Note: You can roast the vegetables and toast the almonds up to a day ahead. Store the vegetables in an airtight container in the refrigerator.

Lay the vegetable mixture in a single layer in a large roasting tin.

Place the vegetable mixture and garlic in a bowl and mix together.

Rub the cut side of the tomato onto one side of each slice of bread.

VEGETABLE FRITTATA WITH HUMMUS AND BLACK OLIVES

Preparation time: 35 minutes +
  cooling time
Total cooking time: 40 minutes
Makes 30 pieces

2 large red capsicums
600 g orange sweet potato,
  cut into 1 cm slices
1/4 cup (60 ml) olive oil
2 leeks, finely sliced
2 cloves garlic, crushed
250 g zucchini, thinly sliced
500 g eggplant, cut into 1 cm
  slices
8 eggs, lightly beaten
2 tablespoons finely chopped
  fresh basil
1 1/4 cups (125 g) grated
  Parmesan
200 g ready-made hummus
black olives, pitted and halved,
  to garnish

1 Cut the capsicums into large pieces, removing the seeds and membrane. Place, skin-side-up, under a hot grill until the skin blackens and blisters. Cool in a plastic bag, then peel.
2 Cook the sweet potato in a saucepan of boiling water for 4–5 minutes, or until just tender. Drain.
3 Heat 1 tablespoon of the oil in a deep round 23 cm frying pan and stir the leek and garlic over medium heat for 1 minute, or until soft. Add the zucchini and cook for 2 minutes, then remove from the pan.
4 Heat the remaining oil in the same pan and cook the eggplant in batches for 2 minutes each side, or until golden. Line the base of the pan with half the eggplant and spread with the leek mixture. Cover with the roasted capsicum, then with the remaining eggplant and finally, the sweet potato.
5 Put the eggs, basil, Parmesan and pepper in a jug, mix well and pour over the vegetables. Cook over low heat for 15 minutes, or until almost cooked. Place the pan under a hot grill for 2–3 minutes, or until golden and cooked. Cool before inverting onto a board. Trim the edges and cut into 30 squares. Top each square with a dollop of hummus and half an olive.

NUTRITION PER PIECE
Protein 4.5 g; Fat 6 g; Carbohydrate 5 g;
Dietary Fibre 2 g; Cholesterol 52 mg;
387 kJ (92 cal)

Lay the roasted capsicum pieces over the leek and zucchini mixture.

Pour the egg mixture over the vegetables so that they are covered.

Cook the frittata under a hot grill until it is golden brown on top.

TEMPURA VEGETABLES WITH WASABI MAYONNAISE

Preparation time: 20 minutes
Total cooking time: 20 minutes
Serves 4–6

Wasabi mayonnaise
2 tablespoons whole-egg
    mayonnaise
3 teaspoons wasabi paste
1/2 teaspoon grated lime rind

2 egg yolks
1 cup (250 ml) chilled soda
    water
1/4 cup (30 g) cornflour
110 g plain flour
1/4 cup (40 g) sesame seeds,
    toasted
oil, for deep-frying
1 small (250 g) eggplant, cut
    into 5 mm rounds
1 large onion, cut into 5 mm
    rounds, with rings intact
300 g orange sweet potato, cut
    into 5 mm rounds

1 To make the wasabi mayonnaise, place all the ingredients in a small bowl and mix together. Transfer to a serving bowl, cover with plastic wrap and refrigerate until ready to use.

2 Place the egg yolks and soda water in a jug and mix lightly with a whisk. Sift the cornflour and flour into a bowl. Add the sesame seeds and a good sprinkling of salt and mix well. Pour the soda water and egg yolk mixture into the flour and stir lightly with chopsticks or a fork until just combined but still lumpy.

3 Fill a deep heavy-based saucepan or wok one third full of oil and heat until a cube of bread dropped into the oil browns in 15 seconds. Dip pairs of the vegetables—eggplant and onion or sweet potato and onion or eggplant and sweet potato—into the batter and cook in batches for 3–4 minutes, or until golden brown and cooked through. Drain on crumpled paper towels and season well with salt. Keep warm, but do not cover or the tempura coating will go soggy.

4 Transfer the tempura to a warmed serving platter and serve immediately with the wasabi mayonnaise.

NUTRITION PER SERVE (6)
Protein 6 g; Fat 14 g; Carbohydrate 30 g; Dietary Fibre 3.5 g; Cholesterol 62 mg; 1112 kJ (266 cal)

Gently stir the combined soda water and egg yolk into the flour mixture.

Dip assorted pairs of the vegetables into the batter.

Deep-fry the battered vegetables until they are golden brown and·cooked through.

SALT AND PEPPER TOFU PUFFS

Preparation time: 15 minutes
Total cooking time: 10 minutes
Serves 4–6

2 x 190 g packets fried tofu
  puffs
2 cups (250 g) cornflour
2 tablespoons salt
1 tablespoon ground white
  pepper
2 teaspoons caster sugar
4 egg whites, lightly beaten
oil, for deep-frying (see Note)
1/2 cup (125 ml) sweet chilli
  sauce
2 tablespoons lemon juice
lemon wedges, to serve

1 Cut the tofu puffs in half and pat dry with paper towels.
2 Place the cornflour, salt, pepper and caster sugar in a large bowl and mix together well.
3 Dip the tofu into the egg white in batches, then toss in the cornflour mixture, shaking off any excess.
4 Fill a deep heavy-based saucepan or wok one third full of oil and heat until a cube of bread dropped into the oil browns in 15 seconds. Cook the tofu in batches for 1–2 minutes, or until crisp. Drain well on crumpled paper towels.
5 Place the sweet chilli sauce and lemon juice in a bowl and mix together well. Serve immediately with the tofu puffs and lemon wedges.

NUTRITION PER SERVE (6)
Protein 55 g; Fat 10 g; Carbohydrate 44 g; Dietary Fibre 1 g; Cholesterol 0 mg; 1135 kJ (270 cal)

COOK'S FILE

Note: Use a good-quality peanut oil to deep-fry the tofu puffs—the flavour will be slightly nutty.

Dip the tofu puffs in the egg white, then in the cornflour, shaking off any excess.

Deep-fry the tofu in batches until crisp, then remove with a slotted spoon.

VEGETARIAN CALIFORNIA ROLLS

Preparation time: 35 minutes +
 15 minutes standing
Total cooking time: 15 minutes
Makes 30

500 g short-grain white rice
¼ cup (60 ml) rice vinegar
1 tablespoon caster sugar
5 nori sheets
1 large Lebanese cucumber, cut
 lengthways into long batons
1 avocado, thinly sliced
1 tablespoon black sesame
 seeds, toasted
30 g pickled ginger slices
½ cup (125 g) whole-egg
 mayonnaise
3 teaspoons wasabi paste
2 teaspoons soy sauce

1 Wash the rice under cold running water, tossing, until the water runs clear. Put the rice and 3 cups (750 ml) water in a saucepan. Bring to the boil over low heat and cook for 5 minutes, or until tunnels form in the rice. Remove from the heat, cover and leave for 15 minutes.

2 Place the vinegar, sugar and 1 teaspoon salt in a small saucepan and stir over low heat until the sugar and salt dissolve.

3 Transfer the rice to a non-metallic bowl and use a wooden spoon to separate the grains. Make a slight well in the centre, slowly stir in the vinegar dressing, then cool a little.

4 To assemble, lay a nori sheet, shiny-side-down, on a bamboo mat or flat surface and spread out one fifth of the rice, leaving a 2 cm border at one end. Arrange one fifth of the cucumber, avocado, sesame seeds and ginger lengthways over the rice, 3 cm from the border. Spread on some of the combined mayonnaise, wasabi and soy sauce and roll to cover the filling. Continue rolling tightly to join the edge, then hold in place for a few seconds. Trim the ends and cut into 2 cm slices. Repeat. Serve with any remaining wasabi mayonnaise.

NUTRITION PER PIECE
Protein 1.5 g; Fat 3 g; Carbohydrate 15 g;
Dietary Fibre 1 g; Cholesterol 1.5 mg;
380 kJ (90 cal)

Cook the rice until tunnels appear, then cover and leave for 15 minutes.

Slowly pour the vinegar dressing into the rice and stir it through.

Spread the wasabi mayonnaise mixture over the vegetables and start rolling.

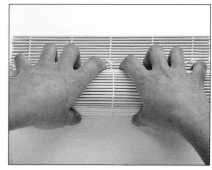

Roll the mat tightly to join the edge, then hold in place for a few seconds.

VIETNAMESE SPRING ROLLS

Preparation time: 30 minutes +
  10 minutes standing
Total cooking time: 10 minutes
Serves 4 (Makes 16)

 **VEGAN**

75 g dried rice vermicelli
200 g firm tofu
1 teaspoon sesame oil
1 tablespoon peanut oil
1 packet 15 cm square rice-
  paper wrappers
1/2 small Lebanese cucumber,
  cut into julienne strips

1/2 carrot, cut into julienne strips
1/2 cup (10 g) fresh mint
1/3 cup (50 g) roasted salted
  cashews, roughly chopped
3 tablespoons hoisin sauce
2 tablespoons kecap manis
1 tablespoon lime juice

1 Place the vermicelli in a bowl, cover with boiling water and leave for 10 minutes. Drain well.
2 Pat the tofu dry and cut into four 2 x 7 cm slices. Heat the oils in a large frying pan and cook the tofu over medium heat for 3 minutes each side, or until golden. Drain on paper towels. Cut each slice into four widthways.

3 Fill a bowl with warm water. Dip one wrapper at a time into the water for about 15 seconds, or until pliable.
4 Place a wrapper on a work surface, top with some vermicelli, tofu, cucumber, carrot, mint and cashews. Roll tightly, folding in the sides and place on a plate, seam-side-down. Cover with a damp cloth and repeat.
5 To make the dipping sauce, place the hoisin sauce, kecap manis and lime juice in a bowl and mix. Serve immediately with the spring rolls.

NUTRITION PER SERVE
Protein 6 g; Fat 12 g; Carbohydrate 16 g; Dietary Fibre 2 g; Cholesterol 0 mg; 580 kJ (136 cal)

Cook the tofu over medium heat, turning once, until golden brown on both sides.

Dip one wrapper at a time into the water until soft and pliable.

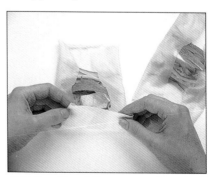

Fold the sides of the wrappers in and roll up tightly, enclosing the filling.

43

Bread, honey, muesli, dried fruit, flour (wholemeal and white), Lebanese bread, fruit loaf, polenta, couscous.

EXCELLENT CARBOHYDRATE SOURCE

Pasta, baked beans, berries, breakfast wheat biscuits, bananas, pumpkin, potatoes, rice, noodles.

VERY GOOD CARBOHYDRATE SOURCE

Tofu, vegetables, milk, fruit, oats, lentils, nuts, yoghurt.

GOOD CARBOHYDRATE SOURCE

Carbohydrates

The principal energy source in the diet is carbohydrate. The vital role carbohydrates play cannot be underestimated as they provide fuel for both the muscles and the brain. Carbohydrates occur in the form of starches and sugars from grains and their products (e.g. flour, bread, pasta) as well as potatoes, legumes, fruits and, to a lesser degree, nuts.

WHAT DO THEY DO?

Carbohydrates break down in the body into glucose and glycogen, both of which are used for energy. The body uses up glucose first and if there is a shortage (for example, during exercise) it converts glycogen, which is stored in the liver, to glucose .

Carbohydrates are generally divided into two categories: simple and complex. A simple carbohydrate is consumed in a form closest to sugar, which takes little breaking down by the body, giving a quick rush of energy, then usually a drop which makes you feel tired or down.

Complex carbohydrates take longer to break down in the body, giving a slower release of sugar and more sustained energy. You probably recognise this phenomenon—you may need a boost, and grab a snack bar or soft drink. Initially you feel better, but soon you will feel worse than you did to start with. Snacking on a complex carbohydrate, such as bread, will give you longer-lasting energy.

FAT OR FICTION?

Carbohydrates have had a bad rap in the past and have been labelled fattening, mainly because of their bulk. But we now know that this is why they are so valuable—they are filling yet usually contain little or no fat. All carbohydrates have less than half the amount of kilojoules per gram than dietary fat and the body converts dietary fat into body fat more efficiently than it does carbohydrates. When you eat carbohydrates your chance of storing their calories as fat is 20% lower than if you eat fat.

Some people argue that fresh or dried fruits are sweet and are therefore high in sugar. This may be so, but fruit also contains valuable nutrients and fibre that the body needs. It is processed cane sugar—found in so many snack foods—that should be avoided. It provides no nutritional value and is often accompanied by lots of fat.

DAILY INTAKE

It is recommended that about 60% of your daily kilojoules should come from carbohydrates. (See the table below for further information.)

VALUE FOR VEGETARIANS

In a vegetarian diet, complex carbohydrates give substance to a meal by filling you up and giving a feeling of satisfaction and repleteness. However, take care what you eat with your carbohydrates. Often a jacket potato is loaded with butter or sour cream, or a pasta dish may have a rich creamy sauce. It is the toppings that make carbohydrates fatty, not the carbohydrates themselves.

Wherever possible, choose carbohydrates that are the least refined. For instance, use brown rice rather than white, go for wholemeal instead of white bread, and rolled oats in the form of porridge or muesli at breakfast rather than processed

SAMPLE MEAL IDEAS
BREAKFAST
- Puffed corn cereal (page 9)
- Porridge
- Mixed berry couscous (page 8)

LUNCH
- Pumpkin and red lentil soup (page 67)
- Sushi
- Wholegrain muffin with tomato

DINNER
- Udon noodle stir-fry (page 58)
- Couscous vegetable loaf (page 71)
- Chunky chickpea and herb dumpling soup (page 66)

SNACKS
- Vietnamese spring rolls (page 43)
- Nuts and dried fruit

(and often high in added sugar) cereals. These wholegrain products are broken down slowly by the body and therefore give a more sustained release of energy.

Complex carbohydrates are particularly important at breakfast to keep you alert and productive throughout the day, which is why breakfast is traditionally cereal and/or toast. Research has shown that by skipping breakfast, students are less attentive and workers less productive. A major danger in missing breakfast is that sugary snacks will be eaten later on in the day.

HOW MUCH CARBOHYDRATE DO I NEED?

The amount of carbohydrate that you need depends on your weight and the amount and level of activity you do. Use this guide to estimate the amount of carbohydrate you should eat each day.

Activity level	Continuous exercise	Carbohydrate/kg body weight per day
Light	< 1 hour/day	4.0–4.5 g
Light–moderate	1 hour/day	4.5–5.5 g
Moderate	1–2 hours/day	5.5–6.5 g
Moderate–heavy	2–4 hours/day	6.5–7.5 g
Heavy	4–5 hours/day	7.5–8.5 g

Example: A man who weighs 90 kg and does less than 1 hour continuous light exercise each day needs 360–405 grams of carbohydrate per day.

MUSHROOM PATE WITH MELBA TOAST

Preparation time: 15 minutes +
  5 hours refrigeration +
  10 minutes cooling
Total cooking time: 20 minutes
Makes 24

50 g butter
1 small onion, chopped
3 cloves garlic, crushed
375 g button mushrooms,
    quartered
1 cup (125 g) slivered almonds,
    toasted
2 tablespoons cream
2 tablespoons finely chopped
    fresh thyme
3 tablespoons finely chopped
    fresh flat-leaf parsley
6 thick slices wholegrain or
    wholemeal bread

1 Heat the butter in a large frying pan. Cook the onion and garlic over medium heat for 2 minutes, or until soft. Increase the heat, add the mushrooms and cook for 5 minutes, or until the mushrooms are soft and most of the liquid has evaporated. Leave to cool for 10 minutes.

2 Place the almonds in a food processor or blender and chop roughly. Add the mushroom mixture and process until smooth. With the motor running, gradually pour in the cream. Stir in the herbs and season with salt and cracked black pepper. Spoon into two 1 cup (250 ml) ramekins and smooth the surface. Cover and refrigerate for 4–5 hours to allow the flavours to develop.

3 To make the toast, preheat the oven to moderate 180°C (350°F/Gas 4).

Toast one side of the bread under a hot grill until golden. Remove the crusts and cut each slice into four triangles. Place on a large oven tray in a single layer, toasted-side-down, and cook for 5–10 minutes, or until crisp.

Remove as they crisp. Spread with pâté and serve immediately.

NUTRITION PER TOAST WITH PATE
Protein 2.5 g; Fat 5.5 g; Carbohydrate 3.5 g; Dietary Fibre 1.5 g; Cholesterol 7.5 mg; 310 kJ (75 cal)

Cook the onion, garlic and mushrooms until the mushrooms are soft.

Blend the almonds and mushroom mixture until smooth.

Spoon the pâté into the ramekins and smooth the surface.

BEETROOT HUMMUS

Preparation time: 15 minutes
Total cooking time: 40 minutes
Serves 8 (Makes 2 cups)

500 g beetroot, trimmed
1/3 cup (80 ml) olive oil
1 large onion, chopped
1 tablespoon ground cumin
400 g can chickpeas, drained
1 tablespoon tahini
1/3 cup (80 g) plain yoghurt
3 cloves garlic, crushed
1/4 cup (60 ml) lemon juice
1/2 cup (125 ml) vegetable
  stock

1 Scrub the beetroot well. Bring a large saucepan of water to the boil over high heat and cook the beetroot for 35–40 minutes, or until soft and cooked through. Drain and cool slightly before peeling.

2 Meanwhile, heat 1 tablespoon of the oil in a frying pan over medium heat and cook the onion for 2–3 minutes, or until soft. Add the cumin and cook for a further 1 minute, or until fragrant.

3 Chop the beetroot and place in a food processor or blender with the onion mixture, chickpeas, tahini, yoghurt, garlic, lemon juice and stock and process until smooth. With the motor running, add the remaining oil in a thin steady stream. Process until the mixture is thoroughly combined. Serve the hummus with Lebanese or Turkish bread.

NUTRITION PER SERVE
Protein 5.5 g; Fat 13 g; Carbohydrate 13 g; Dietary Fibre 5 g; Cholesterol 1.5 mg; 792 kJ (190 cal)

COOK'S FILE

Note: Beetroot hummus can be a great accompaniment to a main meal or is delicious as part of a meze platter with bruschetta or crusty bread. Its vivid colour sparks up any table.
Variation: You can use 500 g of any vegetable to make the hummus. Try carrot or pumpkin.

Drain and cool the beetroots, then peel off the skins.

Cook the onion and cumin for 1 minute, or until fragrant.

Blend all the hummus ingredients until smooth.

BOREKAS

Preparation time: 30 minutes
Total cooking time: 20 minutes
Makes 24

225 g feta, crumbled
200 g cream cheese, slightly
  softened
2 eggs, lightly beaten
¼ teaspoon ground nutmeg
20 sheets filo pastry
60 g butter, melted
¼ cup (40 g) sesame seeds

1 Preheat the oven to moderate 180°C (350°F/Gas 4). Place the feta, cream cheese, egg and nutmeg in a bowl and mix until just combined—the mixture will be lumpy.

2 Work with five sheets of pastry at a time, keeping the rest covered with a damp tea towel. Lay each sheet on a work surface, brush with melted butter and lay them on top of each other. Use a ruler as guidance to cut the filo into six equal strips.

3 Place 1 tablespoon of the filling at one end of a strip, leaving a 1 cm border. Fold the pastry over to enclose the filling and form a triangle. Continue folding the triangle over until you reach the end of the pastry, tucking any excess pastry under. Repeat with the remaining ingredients to make 24 triangles, and place on a lined baking tray.

4 Lightly brush with the remaining melted butter and sprinkle with sesame seeds. Bake for 15–20 minutes, or until puffed and golden.

NUTRITION PER BOREKA
Protein 4.5 g; Fat 8.5 g; Carbohydrate 6.5 g; Dietary Fibre 0.5 g; Cholesterol 35 mg; 505 kJ (120 cal)

Mix together the feta, cream cheese, egg and nutmeg until just combined.

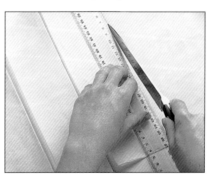

Using a straight edge for guidance, cut the filo sheets into six even strips.

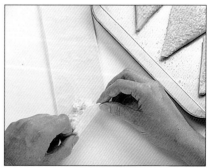

Fold the pastry over the filling, then continue folding until the end.

Using a sharp knife, cut the onions into very thin slices.

Simmer the spicy tomato mixture until it thickens.

Stir the coriander and onion into the batter.

Drop spoonfuls of the batter into the oil and cook in batches until golden.

ONION BHAJIS WITH SPICY TOMATO SAUCE

Preparation time: 30 minutes
Total cooking time: 35 minutes
Makes about 25

Spicy tomato sauce
2–3 red chillies, chopped
1 red capsicum, diced
425 g can chopped tomatoes
2 cloves garlic, finely chopped
2 tablespoons soft brown sugar
1 1/2 tablespoons cider vinegar

1 cup (125 g) plain flour
2 teaspoons baking powder
1/2 teaspoon chilli powder
1/2 teaspoon ground turmeric
1 teaspoon ground cumin
2 eggs, beaten
1 cup (50 g) chopped fresh
   coriander leaves

4 onions, very thinly sliced
oil, for deep-frying

1 To make the sauce, combine all the ingredients with 1/4 cup (60 ml) water in a saucepan. Bring to the boil, then reduce the heat and simmer for 20 minutes, or until the mixture thickens. Remove from the heat.
2 To make the bhajis, sift the flour, baking powder, spices and 1 teaspoon salt into a bowl and make a well in the centre. Gradually add the combined egg and 1/4 cup (60 ml) water, whisking to make a smooth batter. Stir in the coriander and onion.
3 Fill a deep heavy-based saucepan one third full of oil and heat until a cube of bread dropped into the oil browns in 15 seconds. Drop dessertspoons of the mixture into the oil and cook in batches for 90 seconds each side, or until golden. Drain on paper towels. Serve with the sauce.

NUTRITION PER BHAJI
Protein 1.5 g; Fat 2 g; Carbohydrate 7 g; Dietary Fibre 1 g; Cholesterol 14 mg; 218 kJ (52 cal)

TOFU PASTRIES

Preparation time: 30 minutes +
   4 hours refrigeration
Total cooking time: 20 minutes
Serves 4

150 g firm tofu
2 spring onions, chopped
3 teaspoons chopped fresh
   coriander leaves
1/2 teaspoon grated orange rind
2 teaspoons soy sauce
1 tablespoon sweet chilli sauce
2 teaspoons grated fresh ginger
1 teaspoon cornflour
1/4 cup (60 g) sugar

1/2 cup (125 ml) seasoned rice
   vinegar
1 small Lebanese cucumber,
   finely diced
1 small red chilli, thinly sliced
1 spring onion, extra, thinly
   sliced on the diagonal
2 sheets ready-rolled puff pastry
1 egg, lightly beaten

1 Drain the tofu, then pat dry and cut into 1 cm cubes.
2 Put the spring onion, coriander, rind, soy and chilli sauces, ginger, cornflour and tofu in a bowl and gently mix. Cover, then refrigerate for 3–4 hours.
3 To make the dipping sauce, place the sugar and vinegar in a small saucepan and stir over low heat until the sugar dissolves. Remove from the heat and add the cucumber, chilli and extra spring onion. Cool completely.
4 Preheat the oven to hot 220°C (425°F/Gas 7). Cut each pastry sheet into four squares. Drain the filling and divide into eight. Place one portion in the centre of each square and brush the edges with egg. Fold into a triangle and seal the edges with a fork.
5 Put the triangles on two lined baking trays, brush with egg and bake for 15 minutes. Serve with the sauce.

NUTRITION PER SERVE
Protein 9 g; Fat 24 g; Carbohydrate 48 g; Dietary Fibre 2 g; Cholesterol 66 mg; 1946 kJ (464 cal)

Gently mix the tofu and other ingredients together in a bowl.

Remove the saucepan from the heat and add the spring onion, cucumber and chilli.

Fold the pastry to enclose the filling, then seal the edges with a fork.

SWEET POTATO AND LENTIL PASTRY POUCHES

Preparation time: 45 minutes
Total cooking time: 55 minutes
Makes 32

2 tablespoons olive oil
1 large leek, finely chopped
2 cloves garlic, crushed
125 g button mushrooms, roughly chopped
2 teaspoons ground cumin
2 teaspoons ground coriander
1/2 cup (95 g) brown or green lentils
1/2 cup (125 g) red lentils
2 cups (500 ml) vegetable stock
300 g sweet potato, diced
4 tablespoons finely chopped fresh coriander leaves
8 sheets ready-rolled puff pastry
1 egg, lightly beaten
1/2 leek, extra, cut into 5 mm wide strips
200 g plain yoghurt
2 tablespoons grated Lebanese cucumber
1/2 teaspoon soft brown sugar

1 Preheat the oven to moderately hot 200°C (400°F/Gas 6). Heat the oil in a saucepan over medium heat and cook the leek for 2–3 minutes, or until soft. Add the garlic, mushrooms, cumin and ground coriander and cook for 1 minute, or until fragrant.
2 Add the combined lentils and stock and bring to the boil. Reduce the heat and simmer for 20–25 minutes, or until the lentils are cooked through, stirring occasionally. Add the sweet potato in the last 5 minutes.
3 Transfer to a bowl and stir in the coriander. Season to taste. Cool.
4 Cut the pastry sheets into four even squares. Place 1 1/2 tablespoons of filling into the centre of each square and bring the edges together to form a pouch. Pinch together, then tie each pouch with string. Lightly brush with egg and place on lined baking trays. Bake for 20–25 minutes, or until the pastry is puffed and golden.

5 Soak the leek strips in boiling water for 30 seconds. Remove the string and re-tie with a piece of blanched leek. Put the yoghurt, cucumber and sugar in a bowl and mix together well. Serve with the pastry pouches.

NUTRITION PER PASTRY POUCH
Protein 5 g; Fat 11 g; Carbohydrate 20 g; Dietary Fibre 2 g; Cholesterol 17 mg; 835 kJ (200 cal)

Transfer to a bowl and stir in the coriander leaves.

Put the filling in the centre of each square, form a pouch and tie with string.

Blanch the long strips of leek by soaking them for 30 seconds in boiling water.

MAIN MEALS

PUMPKIN TARTS

Preparation time: 20 minutes +
   30 minutes refrigeration
Total cooking time: 30 minutes
Serves 6

2 cups (250 g) plain flour
125 g chilled butter, cut into
   cubes
1/2 cup (125 ml) chilled water
1.2 kg pumpkin, cut into 6 cm
   pieces
1/2 cup (125 g) sour cream or
   cream cheese
sweet chilli sauce, to serve

1 Sift the flour and a pinch of salt into a large bowl and add the chopped butter. Rub the butter into the flour with your fingertips until it resembles fine breadcrumbs. Make a well in the centre, add the water and mix with a flat-bladed knife, using a cutting action, until the mixture comes together in beads. Gently gather the dough together and lift out onto a lightly floured work surface. Press together into a ball, flatten it slightly into a disc, wrap in plastic wrap and refrigerate for 30 minutes.

2 Preheat the oven to moderately hot 200°C (400°F/Gas 6). Divide the pastry into six balls and roll each one out to fit a 10 cm pie dish. Invert the pastry into the pie dishes. Trim the edges and prick the bases all over. Place on a baking tray and bake for 15 minutes, or until lightly golden, pressing down any pastry that puffs up. Cool, then remove from the tins.
3 To make the filling, steam the pumpkin pieces for about 15 minutes, or until tender.
4 Place a tablespoon of sour cream in the middle of each tart and pile the pumpkin pieces on top. Season with salt and cracked black pepper and drizzle with sweet chilli sauce to taste. Return to the oven for a couple of minutes to heat through. Serve immediately with a salad.

NUTRITION PER SERVE
Protein 9 g; Fat 26 g; Carbohydrate 44 g; Dietary Fibre 4 g; Cholesterol 80 mg; 1876 kJ (448 cal)

COOK'S FILE

Note: Try roasting the pumpkin with garlic, olive oil and fresh thyme to add a delicious roasted flavour to the tarts. You can also add texture by adding cumin seeds to the pastry.

Fit the pastry into the 10 cm pie dishes, trim to fit, then prick the bases.

Pile the pumpkin pieces on top of the sour cream.

CHICKPEA PATTIES WITH CARAMELISED ONION

Preparation time: 20 minutes
Total cooking time: 30 minutes
Serves 4

1 tablespoon olive oil
1 red onion, finely chopped
2 cloves garlic, crushed
1 tablespoon ground cumin
2 x 310 g cans chickpeas, drained
¼ cup (30 g) sunflower seeds
½ cup (25 g) finely chopped fresh coriander leaves
2 eggs, lightly beaten

⅔ cup (75 g) besan (chickpea) flour
oil, for shallow-frying
40 g butter
2 red onions, thinly sliced
3 teaspoons soft brown sugar
plain yoghurt, to serve (optional)

1 Heat the oil in a frying pan, add the onion and cook over medium heat for 3 minutes, or until soft. Add the garlic and cumin and cook for 1 minute. Remove from the heat and cool slightly.
2 Blend the chickpeas, sunflower seeds, coriander, egg and onion mixture in a food processor until smooth. Fold in the besan flour and season. Divide the mixture into eight portions and, using floured hands, form into patties. Heat 1 cm oil in a frying pan and cook the patties in two batches over medium heat for 2–3 minutes each side, or until firm. Drain on paper towels. Keep warm.
3 Melt the butter in a small frying pan over medium heat and cook the onion for 10 minutes, stirring occasionally. Add the sugar and cook for 1 minute, or until caramelised. Spoon over the patties with a dollop of yoghurt and serve with a green salad or use to make a burger.

NUTRITION PER SERVE
Protein 35 g; Fat 38 g; Carbohydrate 70 g; Dietary Fibre 23 g; Cholesterol 116 mg; 3170 kJ (757 cal)

Fold the besan flour into the chickpea purée.

Cook the chickpea patties in batches, until firm and golden on both sides.

Stir in the sugar and cook the onion until it is caramelised.

TOFU BURGERS

Preparation time: 25 minutes +
 30 minutes refrigeration
Total cooking time: 30 minutes
Serves 6

1 tablespoon olive oil
1 red onion, finely chopped
200 g Swiss brown mushrooms,
 finely chopped
350 g hard tofu
2 large cloves garlic
3 tablespoons finely chopped
 fresh basil
2 cups (200 g) dry wholemeal
 breadcrumbs
1 egg, lightly beaten
2 tablespoons balsamic vinegar
2 tablespoons sweet chilli sauce
1 1/2 cups (150 g) dry wholemeal
 breadcrumbs, extra
olive oil, for shallow-frying
6 wholemeal or wholegrain
 bread rolls
1/2 cup (125 g) whole-egg
 mayonnaise
100 g semi-dried tomatoes
60 g rocket leaves
sweet chilli sauce, to serve
 (optional)

1 Heat the oil in a frying pan and cook the onion over medium heat for 2–3 minutes, or until soft. Add the mushrooms and cook for a further 2 minutes. Cool slightly.

2 Blend 250 g of the tofu with the garlic and basil in a food processor until smooth. Transfer to a large bowl and stir in the onion mixture, breadcrumbs, egg, vinegar and sweet chilli sauce. Grate the remaining tofu and fold through the mixture, then refrigerate for 30 minutes. Divide the mixture into six and form into patties, pressing together well. Coat them in the extra breadcrumbs.

3 Heat 1 cm oil in a deep frying pan and cook the patties in two batches for 4–5 minutes each side, or until golden. Turn them over carefully to prevent them breaking up. Drain on crumpled paper towels and season with salt.

4 Toast the bread rolls under a hot grill. To assemble, spread the mayonnaise over both sides of each toasted bread roll. On the bottom half of each roll, layer semi-dried tomatoes, a tofu patty and rocket leaves. Drizzle with sweet chilli sauce and top with the other half of the bread roll.

NUTRITION PER SERVE
Protein 23 g; Fat 24 g; Carbohydrate 86 g; Dietary Fibre 10 g; Cholesterol 37 mg; 2740 kJ (653 cal)

Blend the tofu, garlic and basil in a food processor until smooth.

Grate the remaining tofu and fold it into the mixture.

Carefully turn over the tofu patties with an egg flip.

GREEN PILAU WITH CASHEWS

Preparation time: 15 minutes
Total cooking time: 1 hour 10 minutes
Serves 6

 VEGAN

200 g baby English spinach
   leaves
2/3 cup (100 g) cashew nuts,
   chopped
2 tablespoons olive oil
6 spring onions, chopped
1 1/2 cups (300 g) long-grain
   brown rice
2 cloves garlic, finely chopped

1 teaspoon fennel seeds
2 tablespoons lemon juice
2 1/2 cups (625 ml) vegetable
   stock
3 tablespoons chopped fresh mint
3 tablespoons chopped fresh
   flat-leaf parsley

1 Preheat the oven to moderate 180°C (350°F/Gas 4). Shred the spinach into 1 cm slices.
2 Place the cashew nuts on a baking tray and roast for 5–10 minutes, or until golden brown—watch carefully.
3 Heat the oil in a large frying pan and cook the spring onion over medium heat for 2 minutes, or until soft. Add the rice, garlic and fennel seeds and cook, stirring frequently, for 1–2 minutes, or until the rice is evenly coated. Increase the heat to high, add the lemon juice, stock and 1 teaspoon salt and bring to the boil. Reduce to low, cover and cook for 45 minutes without lifting the lid. Remove from the heat and sprinkle with the spinach and herbs. Stand, covered, for 8 minutes, then fork the spinach and herbs through the rice. Season. Serve sprinkled with cashews.

NUTRITION PER SERVE
Protein 6 g; Fat 12 g; Carbohydrate 32 g; Dietary Fibre 3.5 g; Cholesterol 0 mg; 1091 kJ (260 cal)

Shred the baby English spinach leaves into 1 cm slices.

Stir the rice until it is evenly coated and starts to stick to the pan.

Fork the spinach and herbs through the rice mixture.

MUSHROOM MOUSSAKA

Preparation time: 20 minutes
Total cooking time: 1 hour
Serves 4–6

1 eggplant (250 g), cut into
   1 cm slices
1 large potato, cut into 1 cm
   slices
30 g butter
1 onion, finely chopped
2 cloves garlic, finely chopped
500 g flat mushrooms, sliced
400 g can chopped tomatoes
1/2 teaspoon sugar
40 g butter, extra
1/3 cup (40 g) plain flour
2 cups (500 ml) milk
1 egg, lightly beaten
40 g grated Parmesan

1 Preheat the oven to hot 220°C
(425°F/Gas 7). Line a large baking
tray with foil and brush with oil. Put
the eggplant and potato in a single
layer on the tray and sprinkle with
salt and pepper. Bake for 20 minutes.
2 Meanwhile, melt the butter in a
large frying pan over medium heat.
Add the onion and cook, stirring, for
3–4 minutes, or until soft. Add the
garlic and cook for 1 minute, or until
fragrant. Increase the heat to high,
add the mushrooms and stir
continuously for 2–3 minutes, or until
soft. Add the tomato, reduce the heat
and simmer rapidly for 8 minutes, or
until reduced. Stir in the sugar.
3 Melt the extra butter in a large
saucepan over low heat. Add the flour
and cook for 1 minute, or until pale
and foaming. Remove from the heat
and gradually stir in the milk. Return
to the heat and stir constantly until it

boils and thickens. Reduce the heat
and simmer for 2 minutes. Remove
from the heat and, when the bubbles
subside, stir in the egg and Parmesan.
4 Reduce the oven to moderate 180°C
(350°F/Gas 4). Grease a shallow
1.5 litre ovenproof dish. Spoon one
third of the mushroom mixture into
the base of the dish. Cover with potato
and top with half the remaining

mushrooms, then the eggplant. Finish
with the remaining mushrooms, pour
on the sauce and smooth the top. Bake
for 30–35 minutes, or until the edges
bubble. Leave for 10 minutes before
serving.

NUTRITION PER SERVE (6)
Protein 12 g; Fat 16 g; Carbohydrate 18 g;
Dietary Fibre 5 g; Cholesterol 77 mg;
1125 kJ (268 cal)

*Stir the sugar into the thickened vegetable
mixture.*

*Remove the saucepan from the heat and
stir in the egg and Parmesan.*

*Cover the mushroom mixture with the
potato slices.*

UDON NOODLE STIR-FRY

Preparation time: 15 minutes
Total cooking time: 10 minutes
Serves 4

 VEGAN

500 g fresh udon noodles
1 tablespoon oil
6 spring onions, cut into 5 cm
  lengths
3 cloves garlic, crushed
1 tablespoon grated fresh ginger
2 carrots, cut into 5 cm lengths
150 g snow peas, cut in half on
  the diagonal

100 g bean sprouts
500 g choy sum, cut into 5 cm
  lengths
2 tablespoons Japanese soy
  sauce
2 tablespoons mirin
2 tablespoons kecap manis
2 sheets roasted nori, cut into
  thin strips

1 Bring a saucepan of water to the boil, add the noodles and cook for 5 minutes, or until tender and not clumped together. Drain and rinse under hot water.

2 Heat the oil in a wok until hot, then add the spring onion, garlic and ginger. Stir-fry over high heat for 1–2 minutes, or until soft. Add the carrot, snow peas and 1 tablespoon water, toss well, cover and cook for 1–2 minutes, or until the vegetables are just tender.

3 Add the noodles, bean sprouts, choy sum, soy sauce, mirin and kecap manis, then toss until the choy sum is wilted and coated with the sauce. Stir in the nori just before serving.

NUTRITION PER SERVE
Protein 25 g; Fat 7.5 g; Carbohydrate 95 g; Dietary Fibre 13 g; Cholesterol 22 mg; 2330 kJ (557 cal)

Cut the roasted nori sheets into very thin strips.

Cook the udon noodles until they are tender and not clumped together.

Stir-fry the greens, noodles and sauces until well mixed.

TEMPEH STIR-FRY

Preparation time: 15 minutes
Total cooking time: 15 minutes
Serves 4

 VEGAN

1 teaspoon sesame oil
1 tablespoon peanut oil
2 cloves garlic, crushed
1 tablespoon grated fresh
    ginger
1 red chilli, finely sliced
4 spring onions, sliced on
    the diagonal

300 g tempeh, cut into 2 cm
    cubes
500 g baby bok choy leaves
800 g Chinese broccoli, chopped
1/2 cup (125 ml) mushroom
    oyster sauce
2 tablespoons rice vinegar
2 tablespoons fresh coriander
    leaves
1/4 cup (40 g) toasted cashew nuts

1 Heat the oils in a wok over high heat, add the garlic, ginger, chilli and spring onion and cook for 1–2 minutes, or until the onion is soft. Add the

tempeh and cook for 5 minutes, or until golden. Remove and keep warm.
2 Add half the greens and 1 tablespoon water to the wok and cook, covered, for 3–4 minutes, or until wilted. Remove and repeat with the remaining greens and more water.
3 Return the greens and tempeh to the wok, add the sauce and vinegar and warm through. Top with the coriander and nuts. Serve with rice.

NUTRITION PER SERVE
Protein 23 g; Fat 15 g; Carbohydrate 12 g; Dietary Fibre 15 g; Cholesterol 0 mg; 2220 kJ (529 cal)

Stir-fry the garlic, ginger, chilli and spring onion for 1–2 minutes.

Add the tempeh and stir-fry for 5 minutes, or until golden.

Add the greens to the wok in two batches and cook until wilted.

ROAST SWEET POTATO RAVIOLI

Preparation time: 45 minutes
Total cooking time: 1 hour 10 minutes
Serves 6

500 g orange sweet potato, cut
   into large pieces
1/4 cup (60 ml) olive oil
150 g ricotta
1 tablespoon chopped fresh basil
1 clove garlic, crushed
2 tablespoons grated Parmesan
2 x 250 g packets egg won ton
   wrappers
50 g butter
4 spring onions, sliced on the
   diagonal
2 cloves garlic, crushed, extra
300 ml cream
baby basil leaves, to serve

1 Preheat the oven to hot 220°C (425°F/Gas 7). Place the sweet potato on a baking tray and drizzle with oil. Bake for 40 minutes, or until tender.

2 Transfer the sweet potato to a bowl with the ricotta, basil, garlic and Parmesan and mash until smooth.

3 Cover the won ton wrappers with a damp tea towel. Place 2 level teaspoons of the sweet potato mixture into the centre of one wrapper and brush the edges with a little water. Top with another wrapper. Place onto a baking tray lined with baking paper and cover with a tea towel. Repeat with the remaining ingredients to make 60 ravioli, placing a sheet of baking paper between each layer.

4 Melt the butter in a frying pan. Add the spring onion and garlic and cook over medium heat for 1 minute. Add the cream, bring to the boil, then reduce the heat and simmer for 4–5 minutes, or until the cream has reduced and thickened. Keep warm.

5 Bring a large saucepan of water to the boil. Cook the ravioli in batches for 2–4 minutes, or until just tender. Drain, then divide among serving plates. Ladle the hot sauce over the top, garnish with basil leaves and serve immediately.

NUTRITION PER SERVE
Protein 11 g; Fat 40 g; Carbohydrate 35 g; Dietary Fibre 2.5 g; Cholesterol 105 mg; 2351 kJ (560 cal)

Drizzle the sweet potato with oil and bake until golden.

Cover the filling with a won ton wrapper, lining it up with the bottom won ton.

Simmer the cream mixture until it has reduced and thickened.

Cook the ravioli in batches until just tender.

WARM PESTO PASTA SALAD

Preparation time: 20 minutes
Total cooking time: 20 minutes
Serves 4

Pesto
2 cloves garlic, crushed
1 teaspoon sea salt
1/4 cup (40 g) pine nuts, toasted
2 cups (60 g) fresh basil
1/2 cup (50 g) grated Parmesan
1/3 cup (80 ml) extra virgin olive oil

500 g orecchiette or shell pasta
2 tablespoons olive oil
150 g jar capers, drained and patted dry
2 tablespoons extra virgin olive oil
2 cloves garlic, chopped
3 tomatoes, seeded and diced
300 g thin asparagus spears, cut in half and blanched
2 tablespoons balsamic vinegar
200 g rocket, trimmed and cut into 3 cm lengths
shaved Parmesan, to garnish

1 To make the pesto, place the garlic, sea salt and pine nuts in a food processor or blender and process until combined. Add the basil and Parmesan and process until finely minced. With the motor running, add the oil in a thin steady stream and blend until smooth.
2 Cook the pasta in a large saucepan of boiling water until *al dente*, then drain well.
3 Meanwhile, heat the oil in a frying pan, add the capers and fry over high heat, stirring occasionally, for 4–5 minutes, or until crisp. Remove from the pan and drain on crumpled paper towels.
4 In the same frying pan, heat the extra virgin olive oil over medium heat and add the garlic, tomato and asparagus. Cook for 1–2 minutes, or until warmed through, tossing continuously. Stir in the balsamic vinegar.
5 Drain the pasta and transfer to a large serving bowl. Add the pesto and toss, coating the pasta well. Cool slightly. Add the tomato mixture and rocket and season to taste with salt and cracked black pepper. Toss well and sprinkle with the capers and Parmesan. Serve warm.

NUTRITION PER SERVE
Protein 22 g; Fat 45 g; Carbohydrate 90 g; Dietary Fibre 9 g; Cholesterol 12 mg; 3629 kJ (868 cal)

Fry the capers over high heat, stirring occasionally, until crisp.

Add the pesto and toss thoroughly through the pasta.

61

Dietary fibre

Dietary fibre consists of the cellulose and gums found in fruits, vegetables, grains and legumes—there is no fibre at all in any animal products. Fibre is not a nutrient, but rather a substance that ensures proper digestive functioning. It is a group of food components that pass through the stomach and small intestine largely undigested and reach the large intestine virtually unchanged.

SOLUBLE AND INSOLUBLE FIBRE FOODS

Good sources of insoluble fibre
- Cellulose   plant foods, wholegrains, bran, dried fruit, cabbage family
- Lignin   grains, vegetables, fruit
- Hemicellulose   wheat bran, bran cereal

Good sources of soluble fibre
- Pectins   slippery elm, agar, okra, psyllium
- Gums/mucilages   apples, citrus fruit, sugar beet

SOLUBLE AND INSOLUBLE

Dietary fibre may be classified as soluble or insoluble. Soluble fibre is abundant in legumes, oats, barley and most fruits and vegetables. It has the consistency of a gel and tends to slow digestion time, which has the effect of regulating blood sugar—this is particularly important for diabetics.

Insoluble fibre is found in fruit and vegetable skins and the bran coating around grain kernels. Wholegrains (especially wheat, rice and maize), vegetables and nuts are good sources of insoluble fibre. Insoluble fibre passes through the digestive tract largely unchanged and speeds up the passage of material through it.

Foods that provide both types of soluble and insoluble fibre are apples, dried fruits and wholegrains. It is important to have a variety of soluble and insoluble fibre in the diet because each type has a different function.

GETTING ENOUGH FIBRE
- Where possible, leave the skin on fruit and vegetables, such as apples and potatoes.
- Eat whole pieces of fruit and vegetables rather than consuming them as juices.
- Choose wholegrain products such as breads, breakfast cereals, wholemeal pasta and brown rice.
- Drink plenty of water during the day to help digest fibre (6–8 glasses is recommended).
- Snack on fresh or dried fruit rather than biscuits or cakes.

BENEFITS

There are many benefits to a high-fibre diet. Both soluble and insoluble fibre readily absorb water, increasing stool bulk and making it softer and easier to expel. However, dietary fibre is not just important for efficient bodily functions and for comfort; it can also help in the prevention of colon cancer, reduce the risk of diabetes, lower cholesterol (which helps prevent heart disease), reduce the incidence of constipation and haemorrhoids, and help prevent bowel cancer and other bowel disorders. And, the more unrefined the source of fibre, the more effective it is for improved gastrointestinal health.

FIBRE DEFICIENCY

Diets that lack fresh, whole high-fibre foods and instead contain an abundance of refined foods together with animal products (which contain no fibre) have a much higher incidence of diabetes, cardiovascular disease, diverticulitis and bowel and rectal cancer.

FIBRE IS NOT BORING!

There are many misconceptions surrounding the consumption and benefits of fibre. As people turned to 'health foods' in the last few decades, it was thought that large amounts of so-called roughage, such as bran, were needed in the diet. Some of the roughage that was consumed was fairly unpalatable, and this is probably where health foods and vegetarian diets earned a reputation for being wholesome but boring and unappetising.

With the greater knowledge of the last few years, we now realise just how wrong this perception is. Fibre is present in different forms and in many different foods that we probably already consume on a daily basis, so the addition of 'roughage', such as bran, to other foods is not really necessary, and in fact can be detrimental as it can inhibit the metabolism of other nutrients (for example, iron). Eating a variety of sources of fibre is essential as excessive fibre from a single rather than varied source can inhibit the absorption of other nutrients.

BONUS FOR VEGETARIANS

Vegetarians have the edge over meat eaters when it comes to fibre intake, as the bulk of a vegetarian diet, such as cereals and beans, along with fruit and vegetables, are generally rich in fibre. The main thing to remember is to eat a wide variety of foods, thereby ensuring that a range of dietary fibre is consumed—both soluble and insoluble.

DAILY INTAKE

Nutritionists recommend an intake of 30 grams of fibre per day. A typical serving of grains, fruits or vegetables contains between 1–3 grams of dietary fibre. To get the recommended levels of dietary fibre, you need to consume at least 10 or more servings of fibre-containing foods daily. This should be an easy task for most vegetarians.

EXCELLENT DIETARY FIBRE SOURCE Split peas, kidney beans, fruit (e.g. kiwi fruit), vegetables (e.g. pumpkin), wholemeal pasta, haricot beans, garlic, wheat bran.

VERY GOOD DIETARY FIBRE SOURCE Wholemeal bread, dried fruit, peanuts (and other nuts), baked beans, pasta, chickpeas, lentils, raspberries, corn.

GOOD DIETARY FIBRE SOURCE Apples, tempeh, Brussels sprouts, mushrooms, carrots, wholegrain bread, tomatoes, bananas, brown rice, strawberries.

TAMARI ROASTED ALMONDS WITH SPICY GREEN BEANS

Preparation time: 10 minutes
Total cooking time: 25 minutes
Serves 4–6

 VEGAN

1 tablespoon sesame oil
2¹/2 cups (500 g) jasmine rice
2 tablespoons sesame oil, extra
1 long red chilli, seeded and finely chopped
2 cm piece ginger, peeled and grated
2 cloves garlic, crushed

375 g green beans, cut into 5 cm lengths
¹/2 cup (125 ml) hoisin sauce
1 tablespoon soft brown sugar
2 tablespoons mirin
250 g tamari roasted almonds, roughly chopped (see Note)

1 Preheat the oven to moderately hot 200°C (400°F/Gas 6). Heat the oil in a 1.5 litre ovenproof dish. Add the rice and stir until all the grains are coated with oil. Stir in 1 litre boiling water. Cover and bake for 20 minutes, or until all the water is absorbed. Keep warm.
2 Meanwhile, heat the extra oil in a wok or large frying pan and cook the chilli, ginger and garlic for 1 minute, or until lightly browned. Add the beans, hoisin sauce and sugar and stir-fry for 2 minutes. Stir in the mirin and cook for 1 minute, or until the beans are tender but still crunchy.
3 Remove from the heat and stir in the almonds just before serving. Serve on a bed of the rice.

NUTRITION PER SERVE (6)
Protein 15 g; Fat 34 g; Carbohydrate 80 g; Dietary Fibre 9.5 g; Cholesterol 0 mg; 2874 kJ (687 cal)

COOK'S FILE

Note: Tamari roasted almonds are available from health-food stores.

Wearing rubber gloves, remove the seeds from the chilli and finely chop.

Cook the rice in the oven until all the water has been absorbed.

Stir-fry the beans for 2 minutes, coating them in the sauce.

Using a sharp knife, thinly slice 3 large French shallots.

Use a mortar and pestle to crush the Sichuan peppercorns.

Strain the mushrooms, reserving ¹/2 cup (125 ml) of the liquid.

ASIAN BARLEY PILAU

Preparation time: 10 minutes +
  15 minutes standing
Total cooking time: 35 minutes
Serves 4

 **VEGAN**

15 g dried sliced mushrooms
2 cups (500 ml) vegetable
  stock
¹/2 cup (125 ml) dry sherry
1 tablespoon oil
3 large French shallots, thinly
  sliced
2 large cloves garlic, crushed
1 tablespoon grated fresh ginger
1 teaspoon Sichuan peppercorns,
  crushed (see Note)
1¹/2 cups (330 g) pearl barley
500 g choy sum, cut into 5 cm
  lengths
3 teaspoons kecap manis
1 teaspoon sesame oil

1 Place the mushrooms in a bowl and cover with boiling water, then leave for 15 minutes. Strain, reserving ¹/2 cup (125 ml) of the liquid.
2 Bring the stock and sherry to the boil in a saucepan, then reduce the heat, cover and simmer until needed.
3 Heat the oil in a large saucepan and cook the shallots over medium heat for 2–3 minutes, or until soft. Add the garlic, ginger and peppercorns and cook for 1 minute. Add the barley and mushrooms and mix well. Stir in the stock and mushroom liquid, then reduce the heat and simmer, covered, for 25 minutes, or until the liquid evaporates.
4 Meanwhile, steam the choy sum until wilted. Add to the barley mixture. Stir in the kecap manis and sesame oil.

NUTRITION PER SERVE
Protein 13 g; Fat 8.5 g; Carbohydrate 52 g; Dietary Fibre 13 g; Cholesterol 0 mg; 1552 kJ (370 cal)

Simmer the pilau until all the liquid evaporates.

COOK'S FILE

Note: Buy Sichuan peppercorns at Asian food stores.

CHUNKY CHICKPEA AND HERB DUMPLING SOUP

Preparation time: 30 minutes
Total cooking time: 35 minutes
Serves 4

1 tablespoon oil
1 onion, chopped
2 cloves garlic, crushed
2 teaspoons ground cumin
1 teaspoon ground coriander
1/4 teaspoon chilli powder
2 x 300 g cans chickpeas, drained
31/2 cups (875 ml) vegetable stock
2 x 425 g cans chopped tomatoes
1 tablespoon chopped fresh coriander leaves
1 cup (125 g) self-raising flour
25 g butter, chopped
2 tablespoons grated Parmesan
2 tablespoons mixed chopped fresh herbs (chives, flat-leaf parsley and coriander leaves)
1/4 cup (60 ml) milk

1 Heat the oil in a large saucepan, and cook the onion over medium heat for 2–3 minutes, or until soft. Add the garlic, cumin, ground coriander and chilli and cook for 1 minute, or until fragrant. Add the chickpeas, stock and tomato. Bring to the boil, then reduce the heat and simmer, covered, for 10 minutes. Stir in the coriander.

2 To make the dumplings, sift the flour into a bowl and add the chopped butter. Rub the butter into the flour with your fingertips until it resembles fine breadcrumbs. Stir in the cheese and mixed fresh herbs. Make a well in the centre, add the milk and mix with a flat-bladed knife until just combined. Bring together into a rough ball, divide into eight portions and roll into small balls.

3 Add the dumplings to the soup, cover and simmer for 20 minutes, or until a skewer comes out clean when inserted in the centre of the dumplings.

NUTRITION PER SERVE
Protein 17 g; Fat 16 g; Carbohydrate 50 g; Dietary Fibre 12 g; Cholesterol 23 mg; 1767 kJ (422 cal)

Stir the coriander into the simmering chickpea mixture.

Add the milk to the dumpling mixture and mix with a flat-bladed knife.

Pierce the dumplings with a skewer to test if they are cooked.

PUMPKIN AND RED LENTIL SOUP

Preparation time: 15 minutes
Total cooking time: 30 minutes
Serves 4

 VEGAN

1 tablespoon olive oil
1 long red chilli, seeded
   and chopped
1 onion, finely chopped
500 g butternut pumpkin,
   chopped
350 g orange sweet potato,
   chopped

1 litre vegetable stock
1/2 cup (125 g) red lentils
1 tablespoon tahini

1 Heat the oil in a large saucepan over medium heat, add the chilli and onion and cook for 2–3 minutes, or until the onion is soft. Reduce the heat to low, add the pumpkin and sweet potato and cook, covered, for 8 minutes, stirring occasionally.
2 Increase the heat to high, add the stock and bring to the boil. Reduce the heat to low, and simmer, covered, for 10 minutes. Add the lentils and cook, covered, for 7 minutes, or until tender.

3 Transfer the mixture to a blender or food processor, add the tahini and blend until smooth. Return to the saucepan and gently heat until warmed through. Garnish with chilli and serve with Turkish bread.

NUTRITION PER SERVE
Protein 20 g; Fat 25 g; Carbohydrate 36 g; Dietary Fibre 12 g; Cholesterol 0 mg; 1868 kJ (445 cal)

COOK'S FILE

Note: The soup can be made up to a day ahead. Keep covered with plastic wrap in the refrigerator and reheat in a saucepan or in the microwave.

Wearing rubber gloves, remove the seeds and membranes from the chilli and chop.

Stir the pumpkin and sweet potato into the onion mixture.

Blend the soup and tahini in a food processor until smooth.

COCONUT CREPES WITH INDIAN CURRY

Preparation time: 25 minutes
Total cooking time: 45 minutes
Serves 4

½ cup (60 g) plain flour
1 egg
140 ml coconut milk
25 g butter, melted
2 cups (500 g) coconut cream
30 g ghee or butter
1 onion, cut into thin wedges
2 cloves garlic, crushed
1 teaspoon garam masala
1 teaspoon ground cardamom
1 tablespoon Madras curry paste
½ cup (125 ml) vegetable stock
½ cup (125 ml) coconut milk, extra
4 sticks cassia bark
5 cardamom pods
400 g pumpkin, diced
2 small zucchini, halved lengthways and sliced on the diagonal
1 potato, diced
½ cup (80 g) frozen peas
2 teaspoons soft brown sugar
raita, to serve (see Note)

1 Sift the flour into a bowl and gradually whisk in the combined egg, coconut milk and butter until smooth.

2 Heat a 17 cm non-stick crêpe pan or frying pan and grease. Pour some batter into the pan, swirling to thinly coat the base, then pour off any excess. Cook for 30 seconds, or until the edges curl. Turn and brown the other side. Transfer to a plate and line with paper towels. Keep warm. Repeat, making seven more crêpes. (If the batter thickens, add water.)

3 To make the filling, add the coconut cream to a wok and bring to the boil over high heat. Boil for 10 minutes, stirring occasionally, or until it starts to separate.

4 Meanwhile, heat the ghee in a frying pan and cook the onion over high heat for 2–3 minutes, or until soft. Add the garlic and spices and cook for 1 minute, or until fragrant.

5 Add the curry paste to the coconut cream and stir for 3–4 minutes, or until fragrant. Add the stock, extra coconut milk, cassia bark and cardamom pods, bring to the boil and cook for 5 minutes. Stir in the onion mixture, pumpkin, zucchini, potato and peas and simmer for 15 minutes, or until the vegetables are tender and the curry is thick. Stir in the sugar. Remove the cassia bark and cardamom pods. To serve, place ⅓ cup of the filling in the centre of each crêpe and roll up. Keep warm while rolling the remaining crêpes. Serve topped with raita. Spoon on any remaining curry.

NUTRITION PER SERVE
Protein 12 g; Fat 55 g; Carbohydrate 35 g; Dietary Fibre 8.5 g; Cholesterol 80 mg; 2823 kJ (674 cal)

COOK'S FILE

Note: Raita is an Indian mixture of yoghurt and fruit and vegetables.

Cook the crêpes for 30 seconds, or until the edges curl, then turn over.

Cook the coconut cream on the boil for 10 minutes, or until it starts to crack.

GREEN CURRY WITH SWEET POTATO AND EGGPLANT

Preparation time: 15 minutes
Total cooking time: 25 minutes
Serves 4–6

  VEGAN

1 tablespoon oil
1 onion, chopped
1–2 tablespoons green curry
   paste (see Note)
1 eggplant, quartered and sliced
1½ cups (375 ml) coconut milk
1 cup (250 ml) vegetable stock
6 kaffir lime leaves

1 orange sweet potato, cut
   into cubes
2 teaspoons soft brown sugar
2 tablespoons lime juice
2 teaspoons lime rind

1 Heat the oil in a large wok or frying pan. Add the onion and green curry paste and cook, stirring, over medium heat for 3 minutes. Add the eggplant and cook for a further 4–5 minutes, or until softened. Pour in the coconut milk and vegetable stock, bring to the boil, then reduce the heat and simmer for 5 minutes. Add the kaffir lime leaves and sweet potato and cook, stirring occasionally, for 10 minutes, or until the eggplant and sweet potato are very tender.

2 Mix in the sugar, lime juice and lime rind until well combined with the vegetables. Season to taste with salt. Garnish with some fresh coriander leaves and extra kaffir lime leaves if desired, and serve with steamed rice.

NUTRITION PER SERVE (6)
Protein 2.5 g; Fat 17 g; Carbohydrate 10 g; Dietary Fibre 3 g; Cholesterol 0.5 mg; 835 kJ (200 cal)

COOK'S FILE

Note: Make sure you read the label and choose a green curry paste without shrimp paste.

Using a sharp knife, quarter and slice the eggplant.

Stir-fry the onion and curry paste over medium heat for 3 minutes.

Cook, stirring occasionally, until the vegetables are tender.

MUSHROOM NUT ROAST WITH TOMATO SAUCE

Preparation time: 25 minutes
Total cooking time: 50 minutes
Serves 6

2 tablespoons olive oil
1 large onion, diced
2 cloves garlic, crushed
300 g cap mushrooms, finely chopped
200 g cashew nuts
200 g Brazil nuts
1 cup (125 g) grated Cheddar
¼ cup (25 g) grated Parmesan
1 egg, lightly beaten

2 tablespoons chopped fresh chives
1 cup (80 g) fresh wholemeal breadcrumbs
1½ tablespoons olive oil, extra
1 onion, finely chopped, extra
1 clove garlic, crushed, extra
400 g can chopped tomatoes
1 tablespoon tomato paste
1 teaspoon caster sugar

1 Preheat the oven to moderate 180°C (350°F/Gas 4). Grease a 14 x 21 cm tin and line with baking paper. Heat the oil in a frying pan and fry the onion, garlic and mushrooms over medium heat for 2–3 minutes, or until soft. Cool.
2 Finely chop the nuts in a food processor, but do not over-process.
3 Combine the nuts, mushroom mixture, cheeses, egg, chives and breadcrumbs in a bowl. Press into the tin and bake for 45 minutes, or until firm. Stand for 5 minutes, then turn out.
4 Meanwhile, to make the sauce, heat the extra oil in a frying pan and add the extra onion and garlic. Cook over low heat for 5 minutes, or until soft. Add the tomato, tomato paste, sugar and ⅓ cup (80 ml) water. Simmer for 3–5 minutes, or until thick. Season. Serve with the sliced roast.

NUTRITION PER SERVE
Protein 18 g; Fat 44 g; Carbohydrate 16 g; Dietary Fibre 6.5 g; Cholesterol 55 mg; 2195 kJ (525 cal)

Finely chop the cashews and Brazil nuts in a food processor.

Press the nutty mushroom mixture into the prepared tin.

Simmer the tomato mixture until thickened.

COUSCOUS VEGETABLE LOAF

Preparation time: 20 minutes + cooling
time + overnight refrigeration
Total cooking time: 10 minutes
Serves 6

1 litre vegetable stock
500 g instant couscous
30 g butter
3 tablespoons olive oil
2 cloves garlic, crushed
1 onion, finely chopped
1 tablespoon ground coriander
1 teaspoon ground cinnamon
1 teaspoon garam masala
250 g cherry tomatoes, quartered
1 zucchini, diced
130 g can corn kernels, drained
8 large fresh basil leaves
150 g sun-dried capsicums in oil
1 cup (60 g) chopped fresh
    basil, extra
1/3 cup (80 ml) orange juice
1 tablespoon lemon juice
3 tablespoons chopped fresh
    flat-leaf parsley
1 teaspoon honey
1 teaspoon ground cumin

1 Bring the stock to the boil in a saucepan. Place the couscous and butter into a bowl, cover with the stock and leave for 10 minutes.
2 Meanwhile, heat 1 tablespoon of the oil in a large frying pan and cook the garlic and onion over low heat for 5 minutes, or until the onion is soft. Add the spices and cook for 1 minute, or until fragrant. Remove from the pan.
3 Add the remaining oil to the pan and cook the tomatoes, zucchini and corn over high heat until soft.
4 Line a 3 litre loaf tin with plastic wrap, letting it overhang the sides. Form the basil into two flowers on the base of the tin. Drain the capsicums, reserving 2 tablespoons of the oil, then roughly chop. Add the onion mixture, tomato mixture, capsicum and extra basil to the couscous and mix. Cool.
5 Press the mixture into the tin and fold the plastic wrap over to cover. Weigh down with cans of food and refrigerate overnight.
6 To make the dressing, place the remaining ingredients and reserved capsicum oil in a jar with a lid and shake. Turn out the loaf, cut into slices and serve with the dressing.

NUTRITION PER SERVE
Protein 8.5 g; Fat 19 g; Carbohydrate 67 g; Dietary Fibre 5 g; Cholesterol 13 mg; 1985 kJ (474 cal)

Cook the tomatoes, zucchini and corn until softened.

Arrange the basil leaves in the shape of two flowers in the base of the loaf tin.

Mix together the onion mixture, vegetables, capsicum, basil and couscous.

VEGETABLE TART WITH SALSA VERDE

Preparation time: 30 minutes +
   30 minutes refrigeration
Total cooking time: 50 minutes
Serves 6

1³/4 cups (215 g) plain flour
120 g chilled butter, cubed
1/4 cup (60 ml) cream
1–2 tablespoons chilled water
1 large (250 g) Desirée potato,
   cut into 2 cm cubes
1 tablespoon olive oil
2 cloves garlic, crushed
1 red capsicum, cut into cubes
1 red onion, sliced into rings
2 zucchini, sliced
2 tablespoons chopped fresh dill
1 tablespoon chopped fresh
   thyme
1 tablespoon drained baby capers
150 g marinated quartered
   artichoke hearts, drained
2/3 cup (30 g) baby English
   spinach leaves

Salsa verde
1 clove garlic
2 cups (40 g) fresh flat-leaf
   parsley
1/3 cup (80 ml) extra virgin olive
   oil
3 tablespoons chopped fresh dill
1¹/2 tablespoons Dijon mustard
1 tablespoon red wine vinegar
1 tablespoon drained baby capers

1 Sift the flour and 1/2 teaspoon salt into a large bowl. Add the butter and rub it into the flour with your fingertips until it resembles fine breadcrumbs. Add the cream and water and mix with a flat-bladed knife until the mixture comes together in beads. Gather together and lift onto a lightly floured work surface. Press into a ball, then flatten into a disc, wrap in plastic wrap and refrigerate for 30 minutes.

2 Preheat the oven to moderately hot 200°C (400°F/Gas 6). Grease a 27 cm loose-bottomed flan tin. Roll the dough out between 2 sheets of baking paper large enough to line the tin. Remove the paper and invert the pastry into the tin. Use a small pastry ball to press the pastry into the tin, allowing any excess to hang over the side. Roll a rolling pin over the tin, cutting off any excess. Cover the pastry with a piece of crumpled baking paper, then add baking beads. Place the tin on a baking tray and bake for 15–20 minutes. Remove the paper and beads, reduce the heat to moderate 180°C (350°F/Gas 4) and bake for 20 minutes, or until golden.

3 To make the salsa verde, combine all the ingredients in a food processor and process until almost smooth.

4 Boil the potato until just tender. Drain. Heat the oil in a large frying pan and cook the garlic, capsicum and onion over medium heat for 3 minutes, stirring frequently. Add the zucchini, dill, thyme and capers and cook for 3 minutes. Reduce the heat to low, add the potato and artichokes, and heat through. Season to taste.

5 To assemble, spread 1/4 cup (60 ml) of the salsa over the pastry. Spoon the vegetable mixture into the case and drizzle with half the remaining salsa. Pile the spinach in the centre and drizzle with the remaining salsa.

NUTRITION PER SERVE
Protein 7 g; Fat 37 g; Carbohydrate 36 g; Dietary Fibre 4.5 g; Cholesterol 65 mg; 2110 kJ (505 cal)

Mix with a flat-bladed knife until the mixture comes together in beads.

Remove the paper and use a rolling pin to invert the pastry into the tin.

Bake the pastry case until it is dry and golden brown.

Cook the vegetables until the potato and artichokes are heated through.

Spread a little of the salsa verde over the pastry base.

Lay the spinach leaves in the centre of the vegetable mixture.

SPICY VEGETABLE STEW WITH DHAL

Preparation time: 25 minutes +
  2 hours soaking
Total cooking time: 1 hour 35 minutes
Serves 4–6

 VEGAN

Dhal
3/4 cup (165 g) yellow split peas
5 cm piece ginger, grated
2–3 cloves garlic, crushed
1 red chilli, seeded and chopped

3 tomatoes
2 tablespoons oil
1 teaspoon yellow mustard seeds
1 teaspoon cumin seeds
1 teaspoon ground cumin
1/2 teaspoon garam masala
1 red onion, cut into thin wedges
3 slender eggplants, cut into
  2 cm slices
2 carrots, cut into 2 cm slices
1/4 cauliflower, cut into florets
1 1/2 cups (375 ml) vegetable
  stock
2 small zucchini, cut into 3 cm
  slices
1/2 cup (80 g) frozen peas
1/2 cup (15 g) fresh coriander
  leaves

1 To make the dhal, place the split peas in a bowl, cover with water and soak for 2 hours. Drain. Place in a large saucepan with the ginger, garlic, chilli and 3 cups (750 ml) water. Bring to the boil, then reduce the heat and simmer for 45 minutes, or until soft.
2 Score a cross in the base of the tomatoes, soak in boiling water for 2 minutes, then plunge into cold water and peel the skin away from the cross. Remove the seeds and roughly chop.

3 Heat the oil in a large saucepan. Cook the spices over medium heat for 30 seconds, or until fragrant. Add the onion and cook for a further 2 minutes, or until the onion is soft. Stir in the tomato, eggplant, carrot and cauliflower.
4 Add the dhal purée and stock, mix together well and simmer, covered, for

45 minutes, or until the vegetables are tender. Stir occasionally. Add the zucchini and peas during the last 10 minutes of cooking. Stir in the coriander leaves and serve hot.

NUTRITION PER SERVE (6)
Protein 11 g; Fat 7 g; Carbohydrate 20 g;
Dietary Fibre 8.5 g; Cholesterol 17 mg;
780 kJ (186 cal)

Peel the skin away from the cross, then remove the seeds and chop.

Simmer the dhal mixture until the split peas are soft.

Simmer for 45 minutes, or until the vegetables are tender.

SPICY BEANS ON BAKED SWEET POTATO

Preparation time: 20 minutes
Total cooking time: 1 hour 30 minutes
Serves 6

3 evenly-shaped orange sweet
    potatoes (500 g each)
1 tablespoon olive oil
1 large onion, chopped
3 cloves garlic, crushed
2 teaspoons ground cumin
1 teaspoon ground coriander
1/2 teaspoon chilli powder
400 g can chopped tomatoes
1 cup (250 ml) vegetable
    stock
1 large zucchini, cut into
    1.5 cm cubes
1 green capsicum, cut into
    1.5 cm cubes
310 g can corn kernels, drained
2 x 400 g cans red kidney
    beans, rinsed and drained
3 tablespoons chopped fresh
    coriander leaves
sour cream, to serve
grated Cheddar, to serve

1 Preheat the oven to hot 210°C (415°F/Gas 6–7). Rinse the sweet potatoes, then pierce with a small sharp knife. Place them on a baking tray and bake for 1–1½ hours, or until soft when tested with a skewer or sharp knife.
2 Meanwhile, heat the oil in a large saucepan and cook the onion over medium heat for about 5 minutes, stirring occasionally, until very soft and golden. Add the garlic and spices, and cook, stirring, for 1 minute.
3 Add the tomato and stock, stir well, then add the vegetables and beans. Bring to the boil, then reduce the heat

and simmer, partially covered, for 20 minutes. Uncover, increase the heat slightly, and cook for a further 10–15 minutes, or until the liquid has reduced and thickened. Stir in the coriander leaves just before serving.
4 To serve, cut the sweet potatoes in half lengthways. Spoon the vegetable mixture over the top, add a dollop of sour cream and sprinkle with cheese. Serve immediately garnished with fresh coriander.

NUTRITION PER SERVE
Protein 15 g; Fat 5 g; Carbohydrate 72 g; Dietary Fibre 17 g; Cholesterol 0 mg; 1665 kJ (397 cal)

Cook the spicy vegetable mixture until the liquid has reduced.

Cut the cooked sweet potatoes in half lengthways.

LENTIL RISSOLES

Preparation time: 20 minutes +
 40 minutes cooling
Total cooking time: 45 minutes
Serves 4

 VEGAN

1 tablespoon oil
1 onion, finely chopped
2 large cloves garlic, crushed
2 teaspoons ground cumin
1 teaspoon ground coriander
1 small carrot, finely diced
1 cup (250 g) red lentils
1½ cups (120 g) fresh
 wholemeal breadcrumbs
2/3 cup (65 g) walnuts, finely
 chopped
½ cup (80 g) frozen peas
3 tablespoons chopped fresh
 flat-leaf parsley
dry breadcrumbs, for coating
oil, for shallow-frying

1 Heat the oil in a large saucepan with a lid. Cook the onion, garlic, cumin and ground coriander over medium heat for 2 minutes, or until the onion has softened. Stir in the carrot, lentils and 2 cups (500 ml) water. Slowly bring to the boil, then reduce the heat to low and simmer, covered, for 25–30 minutes, or until the lentils are cooked and pulpy, stirring frequently to stop the lentils sticking and burning on the base. Remove the lid during the last 10 minutes of cooking to evaporate any remaining liquid.

2 Transfer the mixture to a large bowl, cover with plastic wrap and cool for 10 minutes. Stir in the fresh breadcrumbs, walnuts, peas and parsley. Form into eight 7 cm round rissoles. Cover and refrigerate for 30 minutes, or until they are firm.

3 Evenly coat the rissoles in dry breadcrumbs, shaking off any excess. Heat 1 cm oil in a deep frying pan, add the rissoles and cook in two batches for 3 minutes each side, or until golden brown. Drain on crumpled paper towels, season with salt and serve with a salad.

NUTRITION PER SERVE
Protein 24 g; Fat 20 g; Carbohydrate 50 g;
Dietary Fibre 14 g; Cholesterol 0 mg;
2014 kJ (480 cal)

Simmer, covered, until the lentils are cooked and pulpy.

With clean hands, form the mixture into eight round rissoles.

FENNEL RISOTTO BALLS WITH CHEESY FILLING

Preparation time: 30 minutes +
  1 hour refrigeration
Total cooking time: 50 minutes
Serves 4–6

1.5 litres vegetable stock
1 tablespoon oil
30 g butter
2 cloves garlic, crushed
1 onion, finely chopped
2 fennel bulbs, finely sliced
1 tablespoon balsamic vinegar
1/2 cup (125 ml) white wine
3 cups (660 g) arborio rice
1/2 cup (50 g) grated Parmesan
1/2 cup (25 g) snipped fresh
  chives
1 egg, lightly beaten
150 g sun-dried tomatoes,
  chopped
100 g mozzarella, diced
1/2 cup (80 g) frozen peas,
  thawed
flour, for dusting
3 eggs, lightly beaten, extra
2 cups (200 g) dry breadcrumbs
oil, for deep-frying

1 Heat the stock in a saucepan, cover and keep at a low simmer.
2 Heat the oil and butter in a large saucepan and cook the garlic and onion over medium heat for 3 minutes, or until soft. Add the fennel and cook for 10 minutes, or until it starts to caramelise. Add the vinegar and wine, increase the heat and boil until the liquid evaporates. Add the rice and stir for 1 minute, or until translucent.
3 Add 1/2 cup (125 ml) hot stock, stirring constantly over medium heat until the liquid is absorbed. Continue adding more stock, 1/2 cup (125 ml) at a time, stirring for 20–25 minutes, or until all the stock is absorbed and the rice is tender and creamy. Stir in the Parmesan, chives, egg and tomato. Transfer to a bowl, cover and cool.
4 Place the mozzarella and peas in a bowl and mash together. Season.
5 With wet hands, shape the risotto into 14 even balls. Flatten each ball out, slightly indenting the centre. Place a heaped teaspoon of the pea mash into the indentation, then shape the rice around the filling to form a ball. Roll each ball in seasoned flour, then dip in the extra egg and roll in breadcrumbs. Place on a foil-covered tray and refrigerate for 30 minutes.
6 Fill a deep heavy-based saucepan one third full of oil and heat until a cube of bread dropped into the oil browns in 15 seconds. Cook the risotto balls in batches for 5 minutes, or until golden and crisp and the cheese has melted inside. Drain on crumpled paper towels and season with salt. If the cheese has not melted, cook the balls on a tray in a moderate 180°C (350°F/Gas 4) oven for 5 minutes. Serve with a salad or vegetables.

NUTRITION PER SERVE (6)
Protein 11 g; Fat 9.5 g; Carbohydrate 48 g; Dietary Fibre 2.5 g; Cholesterol 65 mg; 1377 kJ (329 cal)

Stir the Parmesan, chives, egg and sun-dried tomato into the risotto.

Place a heaped teaspoon of the cheesy pea mixture into the indentation.

LENTIL AND CAULIFLOWER CURRY STACKS

Preparation time: 15 minutes
Total cooking time: 50 minutes
Serves 6

50 g ghee or butter
2 onions, thinly sliced
2 tablespoons Madras curry
    paste
2 cloves garlic, crushed
180 g button mushrooms, sliced
1 litre vegetable stock
300 g brown or green lentils
400 g can chopped tomatoes
2 sticks cassia bark or
    cinnamon
300 g cauliflower, cut into small
    florets
oil, for deep-frying
18 small (8 cm) pappadums
plain yoghurt, to serve
coriander sprigs, to garnish

1 Heat the ghee in a large saucepan over medium heat and cook the onion for 2–3 minutes, or until soft and golden. Add the curry paste, garlic and mushrooms and cook for 2 minutes, or until soft.

2 Add the stock, lentils, tomato and cassia bark and mix well. Bring to the boil and cook for 40 minutes, or until the lentils are tender. Add the cauliflower in the last 10 minutes and cover. If the curry is too wet, continue to cook, uncovered, until the excess liquid has evaporated. Season to taste with salt and cracked black pepper. Remove the cassia bark.

3 Meanwhile, fill a deep heavy-based saucepan one third full of oil and heat until a cube of bread dropped into the oil browns in 15 seconds. Cook the pappadums in batches for 10 seconds, or until golden brown and puffed all over. Drain on crumpled paper towels and season with salt.

4 To assemble, place a pappadum on each serving plate and spoon on about 1/4 cup of the curry. Place a second pappadum on top and spoon on some more curry. Cover with the remaining pappadum and top with a spoonful of yoghurt. Garnish with coriander sprigs and serve immediately. (The pappadums will go soggy if left to stand for too long.)

NUTRITION PER SERVE
Protein 16 g; Fat 13 g; Carbohydrate 23 g; Dietary Fibre 10 g; Cholesterol 24 mg; 1144 kJ (273 cal)

If the curry is too wet, continue cooking to evaporate the excess liquid.

Drop the pappadums into the oil and cook until puffed and golden.

CHILLI, CORN AND RED CAPSICUM SOUP

Preparation time: 20 minutes
Total cooking time: 45 minutes
Serves 4

1 coriander sprig
4 corn cobs
30 g butter
2 red capsicums, diced
1 small onion, finely chopped
1 small red chilli, finely chopped
1 tablespoon plain flour
2 cups (500 ml) vegetable stock
1/2 cup (125 ml) cream

1 Trim the leaves off the coriander and finely chop the root and stems. Cut the kernels off the corn cobs.

2 Heat the butter in a large saucepan over medium heat. Add the corn kernels, capsicum, onion and chilli and stir to coat the vegetables in the butter. Cook, covered, over low heat, stirring occasionally, for 10 minutes, or until the vegetables are soft. Increase the heat to medium and add the coriander root and stem and cook, stirring, for 30 seconds, or until fragrant. Sprinkle with the flour and stir for a further minute. Remove from the heat and gradually add the vegetable stock, stirring together. Add 2 cups (500 ml) water and return to the heat. Bring to the boil, reduce the heat to low and simmer, covered, for 30 minutes, or until the vegetables are tender. Cool slightly.

3 Ladle about 2 cups (500 ml) of the soup into a blender and purée until smooth. Return the purée to the soup in the saucepan, pour in the cream and gently heat until warmed through. Season to taste with salt. Sprinkle with the coriander leaves and serve with grilled cheese on pitta bread.

NUTRITION PER SERVE
Protein 5.5 g; Fat 20 g; Carbohydrate 24 g; Dietary Fibre 4 g; Cholesterol 62 mg; 1269 kJ (303 cal)

Using a sharp knife, cut all the kernels from the corn cob.

Trim the leaves and finely chop the root and stems of the coriander.

Simmer for 30 minutes, or until the vegetables are tender.

Vitamins

VITAMINS	FUNCTIONS	DEFICIENCY SIGNS	VEGETARIAN SOURCES
Vitamin A	Promotes healthy eyes, skin and hair and also maintains the mucous membranes of the lungs and intestines. Improves immunity.	Eye, skin and hair problems, poor night vision, impaired bone growth and increased susceptibility to infections.	Eggs, dairy foods, butter, margarine, apricots and mint.
Beta Carotene (can be converted by the body to Vitamin A)	One of the carotenoids—antioxidants that provide the yellow and orange colours in fresh produce. It improves immunity and protects against the effects of ageing and some cancers.	Increased susceptibility to infections.	Yellow, green, orange and red vegetables and fruit.
Vitamin B group	Provides energy. Important for normal function of the nervous and circulatory system. Needed for healthy skin, hair, nails and eyes.	Anaemia, fatigue, nerve problems, decreased ability to cope with stress, depression, skin problems and greying hair.	Yeast, wholegrain breads and cereals, seeds, nuts, legumes, eggs, milk and leafy green vegetables.
Vitamin B9 (Folate)	Essential for protein synthesis and red blood cell production. Needed to make DNA.	Irritability, insomnia, anaemia. Most common vitamin deficiency.	Brewer's yeast, soy flour, wheat germ, bran, green vegetables, avocados, peanuts, peas, grains.
Vitamin B_{12}	Essential for the functioning of all cells, red blood cell production, bone marrow maintenance, and protein, fat and carbohydrate metabolism.	Anaemia, numbness, unsteady gait, impaired memory, concentration and learning ability, confusion, depression, mental disorders.	Dairy products, microbes (not often found in foods anymore). Vegans may need to take a supplement.
Vitamin C	Produces collagen, which is needed for healthy skin, bones, cartilage and teeth. Improves stress response and helps the body to absorb iron.	Tissue breakdown, easy bleeding and bruising, fatigue, loss of appetite and depression.	Fruit and vegetables (especially citrus fruits, berries, broccoli, pineapple and cabbage).
Vitamin D	Needed to absorb calcium and phosphorus for healthy bones and teeth.	Muscle and bone weakness.	Egg yolk, cheese, margarine, milk, vegetable oils and sprouted seeds.
Vitamin E	Antioxidant. Needed for healthy circulation and healthy muscles, including the heart. Heals scar tissue.	Deficiency is rare. Prevents normal growth.	Egg yolks, corn, nuts, seeds, wholegrain cereals, wheat germ, vegetable oils and margarine.
Vitamin K	Helps to form blood clots. Essential for the formation of protein substances in the bones and kidneys.	Nose bleeds, excessive bleeding.	Broccoli, lettuce, cabbage, spinach, mushrooms, soya beans, potatoes, carrots.

Minerals

MINERALS	FUNCTIONS	DEFICIENCY SIGNS	VEGETARIAN SOURCES
Calcium	Maintains healthy bones and teeth. Regulates nerve and muscle function. Also needed for blood clotting.	Rickets, osteoporosis, osteomalacia, cramps, muscle problems, high blood pressure and heart arrhythmias.	Dairy products, almonds, brazil nuts, egg yolk, soya beans, brewer's yeast, carob, kelp, tofu and dried figs.
Iron	Carries oxygen to the body cells via the blood.	Fatigue, poor circulation, anaemia, dizziness, sore tongue and mouth ulcers.	Legumes, nuts, wholegrain breads and cereals, eggs, molasses, leafy green vegetables, apricots, sunflower seeds, pumpkin seeds and kelp.
Magnesium	Transmits nerve impulses. Helps muscle contraction and relaxation. It also catalyses many essential enzymes and their reactions.	Apathy, weakness, fatigue, anxiety, agitation, confusion, anger, insomnia, muscle tremors, cramps, convulsions and heart rhythm disturbances.	Wholegrain cereals, wheat germ, brewer's yeast, almonds, molasses, kelp, soya beans and leafy green vegetables.
Phosphorus	Essential for the growth of bones and teeth. Helps nutrient absorption, energy production, nerve transmission, metabolism and muscle contraction.	Deficiency is rare. Anxiety, fatigue, muscle weakness, bone pains, osteoporosis, rickets and osteomalacia.	Dairy, eggs, wholegrains, legumes, garlic, nuts and seeds.
Potassium	Maintains nerves, cells and muscles and promotes normal blood pressure and heartbeat.	Apathy, extreme thirst and fatigue.	Vegetables, fruit, avocados, wholegrain cereals, seeds, dates, raisins, nuts, potatoes and pulses.
Selenium	Prevents dry skin and the oxidisation of vitamin E.	Premature ageing, muscle degeneration, liver disease.	Butter, wheat germ, barley, wholewheat bread, garlic, brazil nuts, cider vinegar.
Silicon	Required for formation of new bones. Essential for the synthesis of collagen and elastin and for wound healing and hair and nail growth.	Poor joint formation, gout, stunted growth, brittle nails, bone fractures.	Alfalfa, wholegrain cereals, soya bean meal.
Sodium	Needed for nerves and muscles and regulating the balance of fluid in the body.	Deficiency is rare. Apathy, dehydration, vomiting and cramps.	Salt, yeast extract, bread, cheese, margarine, some take-away foods, olives, celery and peas.
Zinc	Needed for healthy eyes and skin and improves immunity. Essential for taste, smell and appetite. Maintains normal reproduction.	Decreased fertility and libido, poor sense of taste and smell, lack of appetite, poor wound healing, growth retardation and mental lethargy.	Eggs, ginger, yeast, milk, legumes and wholegrain cereals.

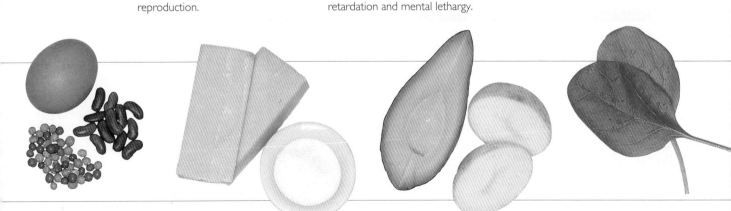

VEGETABLE AND POLENTA PIE

Preparation time: 20 minutes +
  15 minutes standing + refrigeration
Total cooking time: 50 minutes
Serves 6

2 eggplants, thickly sliced
1¹/₃ cups (350 ml) vegetable
  stock
1 cup (150 g) fine polenta
¹/₂ cup (50 g) finely grated
  Parmesan
1 tablespoon olive oil
1 large onion, chopped
2 cloves garlic, crushed
1 large red capsicum, cut into
  1 cm cubes
2 zucchini, thickly sliced
150 g button mushrooms, cut
  into quarters
400 g can chopped tomatoes
3 teaspoons balsamic vinegar
olive oil, for brushing

1 Spread the eggplant in a single layer on a board, and sprinkle with salt. Leave for 15 minutes, then rinse, pat dry and cut into cubes.
2 Line a 22 cm round cake tin with foil. Pour the stock and 1¹/₃ cups (350 ml) water into a saucepan and bring to the boil. Add the polenta in a thin stream and stir over low heat for 5 minutes, or until the liquid is absorbed and the mixture is thick and comes away from the side of the pan.
3 Remove from the heat and stir in the cheese until it melts all through the polenta. Spread into the prepared tin, smoothing the surface as much as possible. Refrigerate until set.
4 Preheat the oven to moderately hot 200°C (400°F/Gas 6). Heat the oil in a

large saucepan with a lid and add the onion. Cook over medium heat, stirring occasionally, for 3 minutes, or until soft. Add the garlic and cook for a further 1 minute. Add the eggplant, capsicum, zucchini, mushrooms and tomato. Bring to the boil, then reduce the heat and simmer, covered, for 20 minutes, or until the vegetables are tender. Stir occasionally to prevent catching on the bottom of the pan. Stir in the vinegar and season.
5 Transfer the vegetable mixture to a

22 cm ovenproof pie dish, piling it up slightly in the centre.
6 Turn out the polenta, peel off the foil and cut into 12 wedges. Arrange smooth-side-down in a single layer, over the vegetables—don't worry about any gaps. Brush lightly with a little olive oil and bake for 20 minutes, or until lightly brown and crisp.

NUTRITION PER SERVE
Protein 8 g; Fat 8.5 g; Carbohydrate 23 g;
Dietary Fibre 4.5 g; Cholesterol 8 mg;
855 kJ (205 cal)

Cook the polenta, stirring, until all the liquid is absorbed and it is very thick.

Reduce the heat and simmer until the vegetables are tender.

Arrange the polenta wedges, smooth-side-down, over the vegetable mixture.

SOYA BEAN MOUSSAKA

Preparation time: 25 minutes
Total cooking time: 1 hour
Serves 4

2 eggplants
1 tablespoon oil
1 onion, finely chopped
2 cloves garlic, crushed
2 ripe tomatoes, peeled, seeded
    and chopped
2 teaspoons tomato paste
1/2 teaspoon dried oregano
1/2 cup (125 ml) dry white wine
300 g can soya beans, rinsed
    and drained
3 tablespoons chopped fresh
    flat-leaf parsley
30 g butter
2 tablespoons plain flour
pinch ground nutmeg
1 1/4 cups (315 ml) milk
1/3 cup (40 g) grated Cheddar

1 Preheat the oven to moderate 180°C (350°F/Gas 4). Cut the eggplants in half lengthways. Spoon out the flesh, leaving a 1.5 cm border and place on a large baking tray, cut-side-up. Use crumpled foil around the sides of the eggplant to help support it.
2 Heat the oil in a large frying pan. Cook the onion and garlic over medium heat for 3 minutes, or until soft. Add the tomato, tomato paste, oregano and wine. Boil for 3 minutes, or until the liquid is reduced and the tomato is soft. Stir in the soya beans and parsley.
3 To make the sauce, melt the butter in a saucepan. Stir in the flour and cook over medium heat for 1 minute, or until pale and foamy. Remove from the heat and gradually stir in the nutmeg and milk. Return to the heat and stir constantly until the sauce boils and thickens. Pour one third of the white sauce into the tomato mixture and stir well.
4 Spoon the mixture into the eggplant shells. Smooth the surface before spreading the remaining sauce evenly over the top and sprinkling with cheese. Bake for 50 minutes, or until cooked through. Serve hot. Serve with a fresh salad, if desired.

NUTRITION PER SERVE
Protein 35 g; Fat 33 g; Carbohydrate 20 g; Dietary Fibre 20 g; Cholesterol 40 mg; 2192 kJ (524 cal)

Scoop out the eggplant flesh, leaving a 1.5 cm border all the way around.

Add the soya beans and parsley to the tomato mixture and stir well.

BEAN AND CAPSICUM STEW

Preparation time: 20 minutes +
overnight soaking
Total cooking time: 1 hour 35 minutes
Serves 4–6

  VEGAN

1 cup (200 g) dried haricot
    beans (see Note)
2 tablespoons olive oil
2 large cloves garlic, crushed
1 red onion, halved and cut into
    thin wedges
1 red capsicum, cut into 1.5 cm
    cubes
1 green capsicum, cut into
    1.5 cm cubes
2 x 400 g cans chopped
    tomatoes
2 tablespoons tomato paste
2 cups (500 ml) vegetable stock
2 tablespoons chopped fresh
    basil
2/3 cup (125 g) Kalamata olives,
    pitted
1–2 teaspoons soft brown sugar

1 Put the beans in a large bowl, cover with cold water and soak overnight. Rinse well, then transfer to a saucepan, cover with cold water and cook for 45 minutes, or until just tender. Drain.
2 Heat the oil in a large saucepan. Cook the garlic and onion over medium heat for 2–3 minutes, or until the onion is soft. Add the red and green capsicums and cook for a further 5 minutes.
3 Stir in the tomato, tomato paste, stock and beans. Simmer, covered, for

40 minutes, or until the beans are cooked through. Stir in the basil, olives and sugar. Season with salt and pepper. Serve hot with crusty bread.

NUTRITION PER SERVE (6)
Protein 10 g; Fat 8 g; Carbohydrate 20 g;
Dietary Fibre 9.5 g; Cholesterol 0 mg;
825 kJ (197 cal)

COOK'S FILE

Note: 1 cup of dried haricot beans yields about 2½ cups cooked beans. You can use 2½ cups tinned haricot or borlotti beans instead if you prefer.

Cook the garlic, onion and capsicum in a large saucepan.

Simmer the mixture for 40 minutes, or until the beans are cooked through.

VEGETABLE CASSEROLE WITH HERB DUMPLINGS

Preparation time: 30 minutes
Total cooking time: 50 minutes
Serves 4

1 tablespoon olive oil
1 large onion, chopped
2 cloves garlic, crushed
2 teaspoons sweet paprika
1 large potato, chopped
1 large carrot, sliced
400 g can chopped tomatoes
1¹/₂ cups (375 ml) vegetable
    stock
400 g orange sweet potato, cut
    into 1.5 cm cubes
150 g broccoli, cut into florets
2 zucchini, thickly sliced
1 cup (125 g) self-raising flour
20 g chilled butter, cut into
    small cubes
2 teaspoons chopped fresh
    flat-leaf parsley
1 teaspoon fresh thyme
1 teaspoon chopped fresh
    rosemary
¹/₃ cup (80 ml) milk
2 tablespoons sour cream

1 Heat the oil in a large saucepan and add the onion. Cook over low heat, stirring occasionally, for 5 minutes, or until soft. Add the garlic and paprika and cook, stirring, for 1 minute.
2 Add the potato, carrot, tomato and stock to the pan. Bring to the boil, then reduce the heat and simmer, covered, for 10 minutes. Add the sweet potato, broccoli and zucchini and simmer for 10 minutes, or until tender. Preheat the oven to moderately hot 200°C (400°F/Gas 6).
3 To make the dumplings, sift the flour and a pinch of salt into a bowl and add the butter. Rub the butter into the flour with your fingertips until it resembles fine breadcrumbs. Stir in the herbs and make a well in the centre. Add the milk, and mix with a flat-bladed knife, using a cutting action, until the mixture comes together in beads. Gather up the dough and lift onto a lightly floured surface, then divide into eight portions. Shape each portion into a ball.
4 Add the sour cream to the casserole. Transfer to a 2 litre ovenproof dish and top with the dumplings. Bake for 20 minutes, or until the dumplings are golden and a skewer comes out clean when inserted in the centre.

NUTRITION PER SERVE
Protein 8 g; Fat 10 g; Carbohydrate 27 g; Dietary Fibre 7.5 g; Cholesterol 16 mg; 967 kJ (230 cal)

Cook all the vegetables until they are tender.

Rub the butter into the flour until it resembles fine breadcrumbs.

Divide the dough into eight equal portions.

SOBA NOODLE SOUP

Preparation time: 15 minutes +
  5 minutes standing
Total cooking time: 10 minutes
Serves 4

 VEGAN

250 g packet soba noodles
2 dried shiitake mushrooms
2 litres vegetable stock
120 g snow peas, cut into thin
  strips
2 small carrots, cut into thin
  5 cm strips
2 cloves garlic, finely chopped

6 spring onions, cut into 5 cm
  lengths and thinly sliced
  lengthways
3 cm piece ginger, cut into
  julienne strips
1/3 cup (80 ml) soy sauce
1/4 cup (60 ml) mirin or sake
1 cup (90 g) bean sprouts

1 Cook the noodles according to the packet instructions. Drain.
2 Soak the mushrooms in 1/2 cup (125 ml) boiling water until soft. Drain, reserving the liquid. Remove the stalk and slice the mushrooms.
3 Combine the vegetable stock, mushrooms, reserved liquid, snow peas, carrot, garlic, spring onion and ginger in a large saucepan. Bring slowly to the boil, then reduce the heat to low and simmer for 5 minutes, or until the vegetables are tender. Add the soy sauce, mirin and bean sprouts. Cook for a further 3 minutes.
4 Divide the noodles among four large serving bowls. Ladle the hot liquid and vegetables over the top and garnish with coriander.

NUTRITION PER SERVE
Protein 13 g; Fat 1.5 g; Carbohydrate 30 g;
Dietary Fibre 6 g; Cholesterol 11 mg;
1124 kJ (270 cal)

Cut the ginger into julienne strips (thin strips the size and shape of matchsticks).

After soaking the mushrooms, drain and finely slice them.

Simmer the vegetables for 5 minutes, or until tender.

VEGETABLE SOUP

Preparation time: 20 minutes +
  overnight soaking
Total cooking time: 1 hour 5 minutes
Serves 6

 VEGAN

1/2 cup (105 g) dried red kidney
  beans or borlotti beans
1 tablespoon olive oil
1 leek, halved lengthways and
  chopped
1 small onion, diced
2 carrots, chopped
2 celery sticks, chopped
1 large zucchini, chopped
1 tablespoon tomato paste
1 litre vegetable stock
400 g pumpkin, cut into 2 cm
  cubes
2 potatoes, cut into 2 cm cubes
3 tablespoons chopped fresh
  flat-leaf parsley

1 Put the beans in a large bowl, cover
with cold water and soak overnight.
Rinse, then transfer to a saucepan,
cover with cold water and cook for
45 minutes, or until just tender. Drain.
2 Meanwhile, heat the oil in a large
saucepan. Add the leek and onion and
cook over medium heat for 2–3 minutes
without browning, or until they start
to soften. Add the carrot, celery and
zucchini and cook for 3–4 minutes.
Add the tomato paste and stir for a
further 1 minute. Pour in the stock
and 1.25 litres water and bring to the
boil. Reduce the heat to low and
simmer for 20 minutes.
3 Add the pumpkin, potato, parsley

*Using a sharp knife, cut the pumpkin
into 2 cm cubes.*

and red kidney beans and simmer for
a further 20 minutes, or until the
vegetables are tender and the beans
are cooked. Season to taste. Serve
immediately with crusty wholemeal or
wholegrain bread.

NUTRITION PER SERVE
Protein 7.5 g; Fat 4 g; Carbohydrate 19 g;
Dietary Fibre 7 g; Cholesterol 0 mg;
600 kJ (143 cal)

COOK'S FILE

Note: To save time, use a 420 g can
of red kidney beans instead of dried.

*Add the vegetables and beans and
simmer until the vegetables are cooked.*

PUMPKIN, BASIL AND RICOTTA LASAGNE

Preparation time: 20 minutes
Total cooking time: 1 hour 25 minutes
Serves 4

650 g pumpkin
2 tablespoons olive oil
500 g ricotta
1/3 cup (50 g) pine nuts, toasted
3/4 cup (35 g) firmly packed
    fresh basil
2 cloves garlic, crushed
1/3 cup (35 g) finely grated
    Parmesan
125 g fresh lasagne sheets

1 1/4 cups (185 g) grated
    mozzarella

1 Preheat the oven to moderate 180°C (350°F/Gas 4). Lightly grease a baking tray. Cut the pumpkin into 1 cm slices and arrange in a single layer on the tray. Brush with oil and cook for 1 hour, or until softened, turning halfway through cooking.
2 Place the ricotta, pine nuts, basil, garlic and Parmesan in a bowl and mix well with a wooden spoon.
3 Brush a square 20 cm ovenproof dish with oil. Cook the pasta according to the packet instructions. Arrange one third of the pasta sheets over the base of the dish. Spread with the

ricotta mixture. Top with half of the remaining lasagne sheets.
4 Arrange the pumpkin evenly over the pasta with as few gaps as possible. Season with salt and cracked black pepper and top with the final layer of pasta sheets. Sprinkle with mozzarella. Bake for 20–25 minutes, or until the cheese is golden. Leave for 10 minutes, then cut into squares.

NUTRITION PER SERVE
Protein 24 g; Fat 32 g; Carbohydrate 33 g; Dietary Fibre 4.5 g; Cholesterol 37 mg; 2166 kJ (517 cal)

COOK'S FILE

Note: If the pasta has no cooking instructions, blanch them one at a time.

Mix together the ricotta, pine nuts, basil, garlic and Parmesan.

Cook the pasta according to the packet instructions until al dente.

Place the pumpkin on top of the lasagne sheet, leaving as few gaps as possible.

ASPARAGUS AND PISTACHIO RISOTTO

Preparation time: 10 minutes
Total cooking time: 30 minutes
Serves 4–6

1 litre vegetable stock
1 cup (250 ml) white wine
1/3 cup (80 ml) extra virgin olive oil
1 red onion, finely chopped
2 cups (440 g) arborio rice
310 g asparagus spears, trimmed and cut into 3 cm pieces
1/2 cup (125 ml) cream
1 cup (100 g) grated Parmesan
1/2 cup (40 g) shelled pistachio nuts, toasted and roughly chopped

1 Heat the stock and wine in a large saucepan, bring to the boil, then reduce the heat, cover and keep at a low simmer.
2 Heat the oil in another large saucepan. Add the onion and cook over medium heat for 3 minutes, or until soft. Add the rice and stir for 1 minute, or until the rice is translucent.
3 Add 1/2 cup (125 ml) hot stock, stirring constantly over medium heat until the liquid is absorbed. Continue adding more stock, 1/2 cup (125 ml) at a time, stirring constantly for 20–25 minutes, or until all the stock is absorbed and the rice is tender and creamy in texture. Add the asparagus during the last 5 minutes of cooking. Remove from the heat.
4 Stand for 2 minutes, stir in the cream and Parmesan and season to taste with salt and black pepper. Serve sprinkled with pistachios.

NUTRITION PER SERVE (6)
Protein 15 g; Fat 30 g; Carbohydrate 60 g; Dietary Fibre 3.5 g; Cholesterol 45 mg; 2425 kJ (580 cal)

Add the rice to the saucepan and stir until it is translucent.

Add a little more stock when most of the liquid has been absorbed.

Stir the cream and Parmesan through the risotto.

MUSHROOMS WITH BEAN PUREE, PUY LENTILS AND RED WINE SAUCE

Preparation time: 30 minutes
Total cooking time: 30 minutes
Serves 4

4 large (10 cm) field mushrooms
1 tablespoon olive oil
1 red onion, cut into thin wedges
1 clove garlic, crushed
1 cup (200 g) puy lentils
3/4 cup (185 ml) red wine
1³/4 cups (440 ml) vegetable stock
1 tablespoon finely chopped fresh flat-leaf parsley
30 g butter
2 cloves garlic, crushed, extra

Bean purée
1 large potato, cut into chunks
2 tablespoons extra virgin olive oil
400 g can cannellini beans, drained and rinsed
2 large cloves garlic, crushed
1 tablespoon vegetable stock

Red wine sauce
2/3 cup (170 ml) red wine
2 tablespoons tomato paste
1¹/2 cups (375 ml) vegetable stock
1 tablespoon soft brown sugar

1 Remove the stalks from the mushrooms and chop them. Heat the oil in a large saucepan and cook the onion over medium heat for 2–3 minutes, or until soft. Add the garlic and mushroom stalks and cook for a further 1 minute. Stir in the lentils, wine and stock and bring to the boil. Reduce the heat and simmer, covered, for 20–25 minutes, stirring occasionally, or until reduced and the lentils are cooked through. If the mixture is too wet, remove the lid and boil until slightly thick. Stir in the parsley and keep warm.

2 Meanwhile, to make the bean purée, bring a small saucepan of water to the boil over high heat and cook the potato for 4–5 minutes, or until tender. Drain and mash with a potato masher or fork until smooth. Stir in half the extra virgin olive oil. Combine the cannellini beans and garlic in a food processor bowl. Add the stock and the remaining oil and process until smooth. Transfer to a bowl and fold in the mashed potato. Keep warm.

3 Melt the butter in a deep frying pan. Add the mushrooms and extra garlic and cook in batches over medium heat for 4 minutes each side, or until tender. Remove and keep warm.

4 To make the red wine sauce, add the red wine to the same frying pan, then scrape the bottom to remove any sediment. Add the combined tomato paste, stock and sugar and bring to the boil. Cook for about 10 minutes, or until reduced and thickened.

5 To assemble, place the mushrooms onto serving plates and top with the bean purée. Spoon on the lentil mixture and drizzle with the red wine sauce. Season and serve immediately.

NUTRITION PER SERVE
Protein 23 g; Fat 23 g; Carbohydrate 42 g; Dietary Fibre 17 g; Cholesterol 20 mg; 2198 kJ (525 cal)

COOK'S FILE

Note: The mushrooms will shrivel if kept warm in the oven—either turn the oven off or find another warm place.

Remove, then very finely chop the mushroom stalks.

Cook the lentils until they are cooked through and the liquid is reduced.

Fold the mashed potato into the cannellini bean purée.

Fry the mushrooms over medium heat until tender, turning once.

Scrape the bottom of the frying pan to remove any sediment stuck to the bottom.

Cook the red wine sauce until it is reduced and thickened.

VEGETABLE TAGINE WITH COUSCOUS

Preparation time: 20 minutes
Total cooking time: 1 hour
Serves 4–6

 VEGAN

2 tablespoons oil
2 onions, chopped
1 teaspoon ground ginger
2 teaspoons ground paprika
2 teaspoons ground cumin
1 cinnamon stick
pinch saffron threads
1.5 kg vegetables, peeled
  and cut into large chunks
  (carrot, eggplant, orange
  sweet potato, parsnip,
  potato, pumpkin)
1/2 preserved lemon, rinsed, pith
  and flesh removed, thinly
  sliced
400 g can peeled tomatoes
1 cup (250 ml) vegetable stock
100 g dried pears, halved
50 g pitted prunes
2 zucchini, cut into large chunks
300 g instant couscous
1 tablespoon olive oil
3 tablespoons chopped fresh
  flat-leaf parsley
1/3 cup (50 g) almonds

1 Preheat the oven to moderate 180°C (350°F/Gas 4). Heat the oil in a large saucepan or ovenproof dish, add the onion and cook over medium heat for 5 minutes, or until soft. Add the spices and cook for 3 minutes.
2 Add the vegetables and cook, stirring, until coated with the spices and the outside begins to soften. Add the lemon, tomatoes, stock, pears and prunes. Cover, transfer to the oven and cook for 30 minutes. Add the zucchini and cook for 15–20 minutes, or until the vegetables are tender.
3 Cover the couscous with the olive oil and 2 cups (500 ml) boiling water and stand until all the water has been absorbed. Flake with a fork.
4 Remove the cinnamon stick from the vegetables, then stir in the parsley.

Serve on a large platter with the couscous formed into a ring and the vegetable tagine in the centre, sprinkled with the almonds.

NUTRITION PER SERVE (6)
Protein 8 g; Fat 15 g; Carbohydrate 33 g; Dietary Fibre 9 g; Cholesterol 0 mg; 1240 kJ (296 cal)

Cook the vegetables until they are coated in spices and the outside starts to soften.

Once all the water has been absorbed, flake the couscous with a fork.

Before serving, remove the cinnamon stick with a pair of tongs.

RICE AND RED LENTIL PILAU

Preparation time: 15 minutes
Total cooking time: 25 minutes
Serves 4–6

 VEGAN

1 tablespoon coriander seeds
1 tablespoon cardamom pods
1 tablespoon cumin seeds
1 teaspoon whole black peppercorns
1 teaspoon whole cloves
1 small cinnamon stick, crushed
1/4 cup (60 ml) oil
1 onion, chopped

3 cloves garlic, chopped
1 cup (200 g) basmati rice
1 cup (250 g) red lentils
3 cups (750 ml) hot vegetable stock
spring onions, thinly sliced on the diagonal, to garnish

1 To make the garam masala, place all the spices in a dry frying pan and shake over medium heat for 1 minute, or until fragrant. Blend in a spice grinder or blender until a fine powder.
2 Heat the oil in a large saucepan. Add the onion, garlic and 3 teaspoons of the garam masala. Cook over medium heat for 3 minutes, or until the onion is soft.
3 Stir in the rice and lentils and cook for 2 minutes. Add the hot stock and stir well. Slowly bring to the boil, then reduce the heat and simmer, covered, for 15–20 minutes, or until the rice is cooked and all the stock has been absorbed. Gently fluff the rice with a fork. Garnish with spring onion.

NUTRITION PER SERVE (6)
Protein 13 g; Fat 11 g; Carbohydrate 42 g; Dietary Fibre 7 g; Cholesterol 0 mg; 1333 kJ (318 cal)

COOK'S FILE

Note: You can use ready-made garam masala instead of making it.

Finely chop all the spices in a spice grinder until they are a fine powder.

Stir the rice and lentils into the onion and garlic mixture.

Simmer, covered, until the rice is cooked and all the stock has been absorbed.

Fat

Fats are our most concentrated dietary energy source. At 37 kilojoules per gram, there are more than double the kilojoules of carbohydrates and protein. This is probably what gives this nutrient group its bad reputation, but, in fact, fat is a vital part of our diet.

THE GOOD NEWS

Everyone needs a certain amount of fat in their body to help with growth and development. Fats supply and help absorb the fat-soluble vitamins A, D, E, K, and they are involved in the conversion of beta-carotene to vitamin A. It is not fat itself that is the problem, rather the quantity and type of fat that we eat.

BAD FATS

The fats most commonly linked to health problems are saturated fats. They are usually solid at room temperature and are derived primarily from animal sources—meat and dairy foods—but they are also found in coconut and palm oils.

The body uses saturated fats mainly for storage, insulation and body heat or energy. An excess consumption of saturated fats in the diet tends to raise blood cholesterol levels and cause fatty deposits in the arteries and blood vessels. This can lead to hardening of the arteries, elevated blood pressure and the formation of blood clots—greatly increasing the risk of heart disease and stroke.

GOOD FATS

The best fats are unsaturated fats, which are usually liquid at room temperature and are derived from vegetable, nut or seed sources. There are two different types of unsaturated fats—monounsaturated fats and polyunsaturated fats.

Monounsaturated fats are generally considered to be good fats, as they do not increase cholesterol levels. They

TIPS FOR REDUCING FAT INTAKE
- Make your meals as filling as possible by choosing foods which take longer to chew and swallow (e.g. whole fruit not fruit juice, whole potatoes, not mashed).
- Don't skip meals or you'll snack later.
- Spread your food intake over the day to keep you calm and full of energy.
- Become aware of times when you are likely to overeat (stressed, bored, free food around) and check your real hunger level before eating.
- Use low-fat plain or skim-milk yoghurt in sauces instead of cream.
- Be careful of hidden fats in snack and processed foods—cakes, biscuits, french fries, potato chips, corn chips, crackers and fast foods. The vegetable oils used in processed foods are the saturated coconut and palm oils.
- Choose polyunsaturated or monounsaturated oil and margarine, which may help lower cholesterol levels.
- Snack on fruits and raw vegetables so you won't feel hungry.

are found in significant amounts in most nuts, olives and olive oil. Other good vegetarian sources are avocados, chickpeas, eggs and sesame seeds.

Polyunsaturated fats are also considered to be good fats. They are found in nuts, grains and seeds and are usually soft or liquid at room temperature. These fats are the most important group of fats as they are the only source of the two essential fatty acids—omega-3 and omega-6 fats.

It is very important to get an adequate intake of omega-3 and omega-6 because they protect against cardiovascular disease, promote healthy skin and are necessary for normal functioning of the nervous and immune systems. Good vegetarian sources of omega-3 are walnuts and some vegetable oils such as soya, canola, mustard seed and flaxseed. Omega-6 can also be found in vegetable oils such as safflower, sunflower, sesame and soya bean, as well as in evening primrose oil.

CHOLESTEROL

Cholesterol is yet another type of fat. It is a wax-like substance present in all animals but not in plants. It is an essential element for good health and is part of every living cell of the human body. It is not necessary to obtain cholesterol from dietary sources as it is manufactured by the liver and adrenal glands to make stress and sex hormones. It is also

required for the nervous system, and it is essential for the breakdown and elimination of fats. Vegetarian foods that are high in cholesterol include egg yolks and dairy foods. Cholesterol intake should be monitored, but research has shown that it is more important to reduce saturated fat intake, which raises cholesterol, than it is to reduce dietary cholesterol itself.

DAILY INTAKE

It is recommended that you try to have no more than about 30–40 g of fat per day (30 g for women and small men, 40 g for men and taller women). Nutritionists estimate that most people living on a Western diet consume twice the amount of fat that they actually need. And vegetarians cannot assume that all vegetarian meals are low in fat, particularly if dairy foods are eaten.

DON'T GO HUNGRY
SNACK IDEAS
- Fresh fruit and vegetables (but go easy on the avocado)
- Fresh fruit and vegetable juices
- Skim milk and low-fat milk drinks; low-fat yoghurt
- Pasta with tomato-based sauces
- Steamed rice with vegetables
- Baked jacket potato with low-fat yoghurt and cheese
- Wholegrain bread and bread rolls
- Rice cakes

HIGH FAT SOURCE

UNSATURATED cashews, pine nuts, olive oil, almonds, walnuts.

SATURATED butter, milk, coconut milk and cream, mayonnaise, (palm oil is another culprit).

MODERATE FAT SOURCE

UNSATURATED soy linseed bread, oats, soya beans, avocados, tofu puffs.

SATURATED eggs, puff pastry, cream, sour cream, cheese.

LOW FAT SOURCE

UNSATURATED bread, tomato paste, fruit, tofu, tempeh, pasta, rice, vegetables.

SATURATED low-fat milk, cottage cheese, yoghurt, filo pastry (without butter).

RATATOUILLE TARTE TARTIN

Preparation time: 45 minutes +
  20 minutes refrigeration
Total cooking time: 50 minutes
Serves 6

1¹/₂ cups (185 g) plain flour
90 g butter, chopped
1 egg
1 tablespoon oil
20 g butter, extra
2 zucchini, halved lengthways
  and sliced
250 g eggplant, cut into 2 cm
  cubes
1 red capsicum, cut into 2 cm
  cubes
1 green capsicum, cut into 2 cm
  cubes
1 large red onion, cut into 2 cm
  cubes
250 g cherry tomatoes, halved
2 tablespoons balsamic vinegar
¹/₂ cup (60 g) grated Cheddar
300 g sour cream
¹/₄ cup (60 g) good-quality pesto

1 Sift the flour into a bowl and add the butter. Rub the butter into the flour with your fingertips until it resembles fine breadcrumbs. Make a well in the centre and add the egg (and 2 tablespoons water if the mixture is too dry). Mix with a flat-bladed knife, using a cutting action, until the mixture comes together in beads. Gather the dough together and lift onto a floured work surface. Press into a ball, flatten slightly into a disc, then wrap in plastic wrap and refrigerate for 20 minutes.
2 Preheat the oven to moderately hot 200°C (400°F/Gas 6). Grease a 25 cm springform tin and line with baking paper. Heat the oil and extra butter in a large frying pan and cook the zucchini, eggplant, capsicums and onion over high heat for 8 minutes, or until just soft. Add the tomatoes and vinegar and cook for 3–4 minutes.
3 Place the tin on a baking tray and neatly lay the vegetables in the tin, then sprinkle with cheese. Roll the dough out between two sheets of baking paper to a 28 cm circle. Remove the paper and invert the pastry into the tin over the filling. Use a spoon handle to tuck the edges of the pastry down the side of the tin. Bake for 30–35 minutes (some liquid will leak out), then stand for 1–2 minutes. Remove from the tin and place on a serving plate, pastry-side-down. Mix the sour cream and pesto together in a small bowl. Serve with the tarte tartin.

NUTRITION PER SERVE
Protein 10 g; Fat 40 g; Carbohydrate 29 g; Dietary Fibre 4.5 g; Cholesterol 144 mg; 2277 kJ (544 cal)

Mix with a flat-bladed knife until the mixture comes together in beads.

Add the cherry tomatoes and balsamic vinegar and cook for 3–4 minutes.

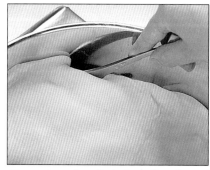

Use a spoon handle to tuck the edges of the pastry down the side of the tin.

EGGPLANT AND SPINACH TERRINE

Preparation time: 1 hour + overnight
 refrigeration
Total cooking time: 55 minutes
Serves 6

3 large red capsicums
1 large old potato, halved
40 g butter
2 cloves garlic, crushed
800 g English spinach leaves,
 shredded
1/4 cup (60 ml) cream
1 egg yolk
1/3 cup (80 ml) olive oil
2 eggplants, cut into 5 mm
 slices lengthways
1 cup (30 g) fresh basil
350 g ricotta
2 cloves garlic, crushed, extra

1 Cut the capsicums into large pieces, removing the seeds and membranes. Cook, skin-side-up, under a hot grill until the skin blisters. Cool, then peel.

2 Preheat the oven to moderate 180°C (350°F/Gas 4). Grease a 1.5 litre terrine and line with baking paper. Bring a saucepan of salted water to the boil and cook the potato for 10 minutes. Drain and cool. Cut into 5 mm slices.

3 Melt the butter in a large saucepan and cook the garlic for 30 seconds. Add the spinach and toss. Steam, covered, over low heat for 2–3 minutes, or until wilted. Cool slightly and place in a food processor or blender and process until smooth. Squeeze out any excess liquid, place in a bowl and stir the cream and egg in well.

4 Heat a chargrill plate over high heat and brush with some of the oil. Cook the eggplant for 2–3 minutes

each side, or until golden, brushing with the remaining oil while cooking.

5 To assemble, arrange one third of the eggplant neatly in the base of the terrine, cutting to fit. Top with a layer of half the capsicum, spinach mixture, basil, all the potato, and all the combined ricotta and garlic. Repeat with the remaining ingredients, finishing with eggplant. Oil a piece of foil and cover the terrine, sealing well.

Place in a baking dish and half fill with water. Bake for 25–30 minutes. Remove from the oven, put a piece of cardboard on top and weigh it down with weights or small food cans. Refrigerate overnight.

6 Turn out and cut into slices.

NUTRITION PER SERVE
Protein 12 g; Fat 30 g; Carbohydrate 8 g; Dietary Fibre 5 g; Cholesterol 88 mg; 1457 kJ (348 cal)

Grill the capsicum pieces until the skin blackens, cool in a plastic bag, then peel.

Blend the spinach mixture in a food processor until smooth.

Spread a layer of the spinach mixture over the second layer of capsicum.

MUSHROOM RISOTTO

Preparation time: 15 minutes
Total cooking time: 40 minutes
Serves 4

1.5 litres vegetable stock
2 cups (500 ml) white wine
2 tablespoons olive oil
60 g butter
2 leeks, thinly sliced
1 kg flat mushrooms, sliced
500 g arborio rice
3/4 cup (75 g) grated Parmesan
3 tablespoons chopped fresh
flat-leaf parsley

balsamic vinegar, to serve
shaved Parmesan, to garnish
fresh flat-leaf parsley, to
garnish

1 Place the stock and wine in a large saucepan, bring to the boil, then reduce the heat to low, cover and keep at a low simmer.
2 Meanwhile, heat the oil and butter in a large saucepan. Add the leek and cook over medium heat for 5 minutes, or until soft and golden. Add the mushrooms to the pan and cook for 5 minutes, or until tender. Add the rice and stir for 1 minute, or until the rice is translucent.

3 Add 1/2 cup (125 ml) hot stock, stirring constantly over medium heat until the liquid is absorbed. Continue adding more stock, 1/2 cup (125 ml) at a time, stirring constantly for 20–25 minutes, or until all the stock is absorbed and the rice is tender and creamy in texture.
4 Stir in the Parmesan and chopped parsley and heat for 1 minute, or until all the cheese is melted. Serve drizzled with balsamic vinegar and top with Parmesan shavings and parsley.

NUTRITION PER SERVE
Protein 26 g; Fat 30 g; Carbohydrate 105 g; Dietary Fibre 11 g; Cholesterol 56 mg; 3299 kJ (788 cal)

Cook the leek and mushrooms in a large saucepan until tender.

Stir the rice constantly until most of the liquid has been absorbed.

Stir the grated Parmesan and parsley into the risotto.

SPINACH AND RICOTTA GNOCCHI

Preparation time: 45 minutes +
1 hour refrigeration
Total cooking time: 15 minutes
Serves 4–6

4 slices white bread
1/2 cup (125 ml) milk
500 g frozen spinach, thawed
250 g ricotta
2 eggs
1/2 cup (50 g) grated Parmesan
1/4 cup (30 g) plain flour
shaved Parmesan, to serve

Garlic butter sauce
100 g butter
2 cloves garlic, crushed
3 tablespoons chopped fresh
basil
1 ripe tomato, diced

1 Remove the crusts from the bread and soak in milk in a shallow dish for 10 minutes. Squeeze out any excess milk from the bread. Squeeze out any excess liquid from the spinach.
2 Place the bread, spinach, ricotta, eggs and Parmesan in a bowl and mix thoroughly. Refrigerate, covered, for 1 hour. Fold the flour in well.
3 Lightly dust your hands in flour and roll heaped teaspoons of the mixture into dumplings. Lower batches of the gnocchi into a large saucepan of boiling salted water. Cook for about 2 minutes, or until the gnocchi rise to the surface. Transfer to a serving plate and keep warm.
4 To make the sauce, combine all the ingredients in a small saucepan and cook over medium heat for 3 minutes, or until the butter is nutty brown. Drizzle over the gnocchi and sprinkle with the shaved Parmesan.

NUTRITION PER SERVE (6)
Protein 17 g; Fat 26 g; Carbohydrate 16 g; Dietary Fibre 5 g; Cholesterol 137 mg; 1504 kJ (360 cal)

Gently squeeze out any excess milk from the bread.

With floured hands, roll teaspoons of the mixture into dumplings.

Cook the gnocchi in batches until they rise to the surface.

VIETNAMESE SALAD

Preparation time: 30 minutes +
  10 minutes standing + 30 minutes
  refrigeration
Total cooking time: Nil
Serves 4–6

 VEGAN

200 g dried rice vermicelli
1/2 cup (10 g) firmly packed torn
  fresh Vietnamese mint
1/2 cup (15 g) firmly packed
  fresh coriander leaves
1/2 red onion, cut into thin
  wedges
1 green mango, cut into julienne
  strips

1 Lebanese cucumber, halved
  lengthways and thinly sliced
  on the diagonal
1 cup (140 g) crushed peanuts

Lemon grass dressing
1/2 cup (125 ml) lime juice
1 tablespoon shaved palm sugar
1/4 cup (60 ml) seasoned rice
  vinegar
2 stems lemon grass, finely
  chopped
2 red chillies, seeded and finely
  chopped
3 kaffir lime leaves, shredded

1 Place the rice vermicelli in a bowl
and cover with boiling water. Leave

for 10 minutes, or until soft, then
drain, rinse under cold water and cut
into short lengths.
2 Place the vermicelli, mint,
coriander, onion, mango, cucumber
and three-quarters of the nuts in a
large bowl and toss together.
3 To make the dressing, place all the
ingredients in a jar with a lid and
shake together.
4 Toss the dressing through the
salad and refrigerate for 30 minutes.
Sprinkle with the remaining nuts just
before serving.

NUTRITION PER SERVE (6)
Protein 6.5 g; Fat 13 g; Carbohydrate 19 g;
Dietary Fibre 3 g; Cholesterol 0 mg;
926 kJ (221 cal)

Cut the green mango into julienne strips
(the size and shape of matchsticks).

Using scissors, cut the rice vermicelli into
short lengths.

Toss the salad ingredients together in a
large bowl.

PHAD THAI

Preparation time: 20 minutes
Total cooking time: 15 minutes
Serves 4

400 g flat rice-stick noodles
2 tablespoons peanut oil
2 eggs, lightly beaten
1 onion, cut into thin wedges
2 cloves garlic, crushed
1 small red capsicum, cut into
 thin strips
100 g fried tofu, cut into 5 mm
 wide strips
6 spring onions, thinly sliced on
 the diagonal

¹/₂ cup (25 g) chopped fresh
 coriander leaves
¹/₄ cup (60 ml) soy sauce
2 tablespoons lime juice
1 tablespoon soft brown sugar
2 teaspoons sambal oelek
1 cup (90 g) bean shoots
¹/₄ cup (40 g) chopped roasted
 unsalted peanuts

1 Cook the noodles in a saucepan of boiling water for 5–10 minutes, or until tender. Drain and set aside.
2 Heat a wok over high heat and add enough peanut oil to coat the bottom and side. When smoking, add the egg and swirl to form a thin omelette. Cook for 30 seconds, or until just set. Roll up, remove and thinly slice.
3 Heat the remaining oil in the wok. Add the onion, garlic and capsicum and cook over high heat for 2–3 minutes, or until the onion softens. Add the noodles, tossing well. Stir in the omelette, tofu, spring onion and half the coriander.
4 Pour in the combined soy sauce, lime juice, sugar and sambal oelek, then toss to coat the noodles. Sprinkle with the bean shoots and top with roasted peanuts and the remaining coriander. Serve immediately.

NUTRITION PER SERVE
Protein 13 g; Fat 21 g; Carbohydrate 34 g;
Dietary Fibre 5 g; Cholesterol 90 mg;
1565 kJ (375 cal)

Using a sharp knife, slice the fried tofu into 5 mm wide strips.

Once the omelette is golden and set, carefully roll it up.

Stir in the omelette, tofu, spring onion and coriander.

BROWN RICE AND CASHEW PATTIES WITH CORIANDER SAMBAL

Preparation time: 30 minutes +
overnight soaking + 30 minutes
refrigeration
Total cooking time: 2 hours 5 minutes
Serves 8

250 g dried chickpeas
3 cups (660 g) instant brown
  rice (see Note)
1 tablespoon oil
1 onion, finely chopped
125 g roasted cashew paste
1 egg
60 g tahini
1 teaspoon ground cumin
1 teaspoon ground turmeric
2 tablespoons tamari
1 tablespoon lemon juice
1 vegetable stock cube
1 small carrot, grated
1/2 cup (40 g) fresh wholemeal
  breadcrumbs
oil, for shallow-frying
2 tablespoons oil, extra
310 g bok choy, trimmed and
  washed
1/4 cup (60 ml) tamari, extra

Coriander and coconut sambal
90 g fresh coriander leaves
1 clove garlic, chopped
1 small fresh green chilli,
  seeded and finely chopped
1 teaspoon garam masala
2 tablespoons lime juice
1/4 cup (15 g) shredded coconut

1 Soak the chickpeas in cold water overnight. Drain. Place in a large saucepan and cover with water. Bring to the boil and cook for 1–1 1/2 hours, or until cooked. Drain, reserving 2 tablespoons of the liquid.

2 Meanwhile, bring a saucepan of water to the boil and cook the rice over medium heat for 10–12 minutes, or until tender. Rinse well and drain. Keep warm.

3 Heat the oil in a frying pan and cook the onion for 2–3 minutes, or until golden. Set aside.

4 Mix the chickpeas, cashew paste, egg, tahini, cumin, turmeric, tamari, lemon juice, stock cube and reserved chickpea liquid in a food processor until smooth. Transfer to a large bowl and add the rice, onion, carrot and breadcrumbs and mix well. Divide the mixture into 16 even portions and form into patties about 1.5 cm thick. Refrigerate for 30 minutes.

5 To make the sambal, finely chop all the ingredients in a food processor. Refrigerate until ready to use.

6 To cook the patties, heat the oil in a large deep frying pan over medium heat and cook in batches for 3–4 minutes each side, or until golden and cooked through. Remove and keep warm. Wipe with a paper towel. In the same pan, heat the extra oil and add the bok choy and cook, tossing, for 1–2 minutes, or until wilted. Pour on the extra tamari and toss through. Place the bok choy on eight serving plates and top with two patties. Spoon a dollop of chilled sambal on top and serve immediately.

NUTRITION PER SERVE
Protein 17 g; Fat 17 g; Carbohydrate 80 g; Dietary Fibre 11 g; Cholesterol 23 mg; 2294 kJ (548 cal)

COOK'S FILE

Note: The rice has been cooked, then dehydrated so it takes less time to cook than normal rice.

Cook the rice over medium heat until tender.

Mix the chickpeas and other ingredients in a food processor until smooth.

Using your hands, form the mixture into 16 even patties about 1.5 cm thick.

Finely chop all the sambal ingredients in a food processor.

Cook the patties in batches until golden brown and cooked through.

Cook the bok choy until wilted, then toss through the extra tamari.

HIGH-TOP VEGETABLE PIE

Preparation time: 25 minutes +
  20 minutes refrigeration
Total cooking time: 1 hour 30 minutes
Serves 6

Pastry
1 cup (125 g) plain flour
60 g chilled butter, chopped
1 egg yolk
2 teaspoons poppy seeds
1–2 tablespoons iced water

30 g butter
2 tablespoons oil
1 onion, cut into thin wedges
1 leek, sliced
3 potatoes, cut into large chunks
300 g orange sweet potato, cut
  into large chunks
300 g pumpkin, cut into large
  chunks
200 g swede, peeled and cut
  into large chunks
1 cup (250 ml) vegetable stock
1 red capsicum, cut into large
  pieces
200 g broccoli, cut into large
  florets
2 zucchini, cut into large pieces
1 cup (125 g) grated vintage
  peppercorn Cheddar

1 Preheat the oven to moderately hot 200°C (400°F/Gas 6). To make the pastry, sift the flour into a large bowl and add the butter. Rub the butter in with your fingertips until it resembles fine breadcrumbs. Make a well in the centre and add the egg yolk, poppy seeds and water and mix with a flat-bladed knife, using a cutting action, until the mixture comes together in beads. Gently gather the dough together and lift out onto a lightly floured work surface. Press the dough together into a ball and flatten it slightly into a disc, wrap in plastic wrap and refrigerate for 20 minutes.
2 Roll the dough out between two sheets of baking paper, then remove the top sheet and invert the pastry over a 23 cm pie plate. Use a small ball of pastry to help press the pastry into the plate, allowing any excess to hang over the sides. Use a sharp knife to trim away any excess pastry. Prick

the base with a fork and bake for 15–20 minutes, or until dry and golden.
3 To make the filling, heat the butter and oil in a large saucepan, add the onion and leek and cook over medium heat for 5 minutes, or until soft and golden. Add the potato, sweet potato, pumpkin and swede and cook, stirring occasionally, until the vegetables start to soften. Add the stock and simmer for 30 minutes.
4 Add the remaining vegetables, reduce the heat and simmer for

20 minutes, or until the vegetables are soft—some may break up slightly. The mixture should be just mushy. Season to taste with salt and pepper. Allow the mixture to cool a little.
5 Spoon the mixture into the shell, sprinkle with cheese and cook under a medium grill for 5–10 minutes, or until the cheese is golden brown.

NUTRITION PER SERVE
Protein 14 g; Fat 27 g; Carbohydrate 32 g; Dietary Fibre 6.5 g; Cholesterol 90 mg; 1790 kJ (428 cal)

Prick the base of the pastry all over with a fork and bake until dry and golden.

Cook the vegetables until they are very soft when tested with a knife.

SPINACH PIE

Preparation time: 45 minutes +
  1 hour refrigeration
Total cooking time: 55 minutes
Serves 6

Pastry
2 cups (250 g) plain flour
30 g chilled butter, chopped
1/4 cup (60 ml) olive oil

Filling
500 g English spinach leaves
2 teaspoons olive oil
1 onion, finely chopped
3 spring onions, finely chopped
200 g feta, crumbled
2 tablespoons chopped fresh
  flat-leaf parsley
1 tablespoon chopped fresh dill
2 tablespoons grated kefalotyri
  cheese
1/4 cup (45 g) cooked white rice
1/4 cup (40 g) pine nuts, toasted
  and roughly chopped
1/4 teaspoon ground nutmeg
1/2 teaspoon ground cumin
3 eggs, lightly beaten

1 Lightly grease a shallow 17 x 26 cm tin. To make the pastry, sift the flour and 1/2 teaspoon salt into a large bowl. Add the butter and rub in with your fingertips until the mixture resembles fine breadcrumbs. Make a well in the centre and add the oil. Using your hands, mix together. Add 1/2 cup (125 ml) warm water and mix with a flat-bladed knife, using a cutting action until the mixture comes together in beads. Gently gather the dough together and lift out onto a lightly floured surface. Press into a ball and flatten into a disc. Wrap in plastic wrap and refrigerate for 1 hour.
2 Trim and wash the spinach, then coarsely chop the leaves and stems. Wrap in a tea towel and squeeze out as much moisture as possible. Heat the oil in a frying pan, add the onion and spring onion and cook over low heat, without browning, for 5 minutes, or until softened. Place in a bowl with the spinach and the remaining filling ingredients and mix well. Season.
3 Preheat the oven to moderately hot 200°C (400°F/Gas 6). Roll out just over half the pastry between two sheets of

baking paper, remove the top sheet and invert the pastry into the tin. Use a small ball of pastry to help press the pastry into the tin, allowing any excess to hang over the sides. Spoon the filling into the tin. Roll out the remaining pastry until large enough to cover the top. Place over the filling and press the two pastry edges firmly together to seal. Use a small sharp knife to trim away any extra pastry. Brush the top with a little oil, then score three strips lengthways, then on

the diagonal to make a diamond pattern on the surface. Make two slits in the top to allow steam to escape.
4 Bake for 45–50 minutes, covering with foil if the surface becomes too brown. The pie is cooked when it slides when the tin is gently shaken. Turn out onto a rack for 10 minutes, then cut into pieces and serve.

NUTRITION PER SERVE
Protein 19 g; Fat 33 g; Carbohydrate 39 g; Dietary Fibre 5 g; Cholesterol 133 mg; 2207 kJ (527 cal)

Spoon the spinach filling into the pastry-lined tin.

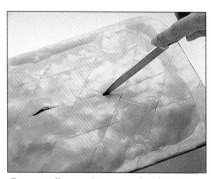

Score a diamond pattern in the pastry, then make two slits so steam can escape.

FETA, TOMATO AND OLIVE PIZZA

Preparation time: 30 minutes +
  1 hour rising
Total cooking time: 50 minutes
Serves 4–6

Pizza base
7 g sachet dry yeast
3/4 cup (90 g) plain flour
**3/4 cup (110 g) wholemeal plain
  flour**
1 tablespoon olive oil

1 tablespoon oil
2 onions, sliced
2 teaspoons soft brown sugar
1–2 tablespoons olive paste
250 g cherry tomatoes, halved
200 g feta, crumbled
**1/4 cup (7 g) loosely packed
  fresh basil, shredded**

1 To make the dough, place the yeast and flours in a large bowl and mix well. Make a well in the centre and add the olive oil and 1/2 cup (125 ml) warm water. Mix well, adding a little more water if the dough seems too dry, then gather together with your hands. Turn out onto a lightly floured surface and knead for 5 minutes. Place the dough into a lightly oiled bowl, cover with plastic wrap and leave in a draught-free place for 1 hour.
2 Meanwhile, heat the oil in a frying pan and cook the onion over medium–low heat for 20 minutes, stirring regularly. Add the sugar and cook, stirring, for 1–2 minutes, or until caramelised. Set aside to cool.
3 Preheat the oven to hot 220°C (425°F/Gas 7). Punch down the dough and knead for 1 minute. Roll out to a 30 cm round (it will shrink as you roll it), then tuck 1 cm of the dough under to create a rim. Sprinkle an oven tray lightly with polenta or brush with oil, and place the dough on the tray.
4 Spread the paste over the dough, leaving a 1 cm border, then top with the onion. Arrange the tomato halves over the onion, and sprinkle with feta and basil. Bake for 25 minutes.

NUTRITION PER SERVE (6)
Protein 11 g; Fat 15 g; Carbohydrate 25 g; Dietary Fibre 4 g; Cholesterol 23 mg; 1170 kJ (279 cal)

Pour the olive oil and 1/2 cup (125 ml) warm water into the well.

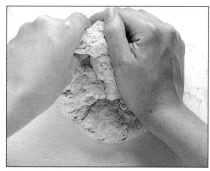
Turn the dough out onto a lightly floured surface and knead.

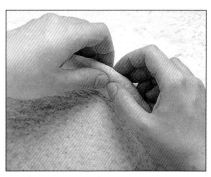
Fold the edges of the dough under to make a rim.

Sprinkle the feta over the onion and tomato.

ROAST VEGETABLE TART

Preparation time: 30 minutes
Total cooking time: 1 hour 45 minutes
Serves 4–6

2 slender eggplants, halved and
  cut into thick slices
350 g pumpkin, cut into large
  pieces
2 zucchini, halved and cut into
  thick slices
1–2 tablespoons olive oil
1 large red capsicum, chopped
1 teaspoon olive oil, extra
1 red onion, cut into thin wedges
1 tablespoon Korma curry paste
plain yoghurt, to serve

Pastry
1½ cups (185 g) plain flour
125 g butter, chopped
⅔ cup (100 g) roasted cashews,
  finely chopped
1 teaspoon cumin seeds
2–3 tablespoons chilled water

1 Preheat the oven to moderately hot 200°C (400°F/Gas 6). Put the eggplant, pumpkin and zucchini on a lined oven tray, then brush with oil and bake for

30 minutes. Turn, add the capsicum and bake for 30 minutes. Cool.
2 Meanwhile, heat the extra oil in a frying pan and cook the onion for 2–3 minutes, or until soft. Add the curry paste and cook, stirring, for 1 minute, or until fragrant and well mixed. Cool. Reduce the oven to moderate 180°C (350°F/Gas 4).
3 To make the pastry, sift the flour into a large bowl and add the butter. Rub the butter into the flour with your fingertips until it resembles fine breadcrumbs. Stir in the cashews and cumin seeds. Make a well in the centre and add the water. Mix with a flat-bladed knife, using a cutting action, until the mixture comes together in

beads. Gather the dough together and lift out onto a sheet of baking paper. Flatten to a disc, then roll out to a circle about 35 cm in diameter.
4 Lift onto an oven tray and spread the onion mixture over the pastry, leaving a 6 cm border. Arrange the other vegetables over the onion, piling them slightly higher in the centre. Working your way around, fold the edge of the pastry in pleats over the vegetables. Bake for 45 minutes, or until the pastry is golden. Serve immediately with plain yoghurt.

NUTRITION PER SERVE (6)
Protein 9 g; Fat 34 g; Carbohydrate 33 g; Dietary Fibre 5 g; Cholesterol 54 mg; 1959 kJ (470 cal)

Spread the onion mixture over the pastry, leaving a 6 cm border.

Fold the edge of the pastry over the vegetables in rough pleats.

VEGETABLE AND TOFU KEBABS

Preparation time: 40 minutes +
  30 minutes marinating
Total cooking time: 30 minutes
Serves 4

500 g firm tofu, cut into 2 cm
    cubes
1 red capsicum, cut into 2 cm
    cubes
3 zucchini, cut into 2 cm lengths
4 small onions, cut into quarters
300 g button mushrooms, cut
    into quarters
1/2 cup (125 ml) tamari
1/2 cup (125 ml) sesame oil
3 cm piece ginger, peeled and
    grated
1/2 cup (175 g) honey
1 tablespoon sesame oil, extra
1 small onion, finely chopped
1 clove garlic, crushed
2 teaspoons chilli paste
1 cup (250 g) smooth peanut
    butter
1 cup (250 ml) coconut milk
1 tablespoon soft brown sugar
1 tablespoon tamari
1 tablespoon lemon juice
1/4 cup (40 g) peanuts, roasted
    and chopped
1/4 cup (40 g) sesame seeds,
    toasted

1 Preheat the oven to hot 220°C (425°F/Gas 7). Soak 12 bamboo skewers in water for 2 hours. Thread the tofu, capsicum, zucchini, onions and mushrooms alternately onto the skewers. Lay out in a large flat dish.
2 Combine the tamari, oil, ginger and honey in a non-metallic bowl. Pour over the kebabs. Leave for 30 minutes.

Cook on a hot barbecue or chargrill, basting and turning, for 10–15 minutes, or until tender. Keep warm.
3 To make the peanut sauce, heat the extra oil in a large frying pan over medium heat and cook the onion, garlic and chilli paste for 1–2 minutes, or until the onion is soft. Reduce the heat, add the peanut butter, coconut milk, sugar, tamari and lemon juice

and stir. Bring to the boil, then reduce the heat and simmer for 10 minutes, or until just thick. Stir in the peanuts. If the sauce is too thick, add water.
4 Drizzle peanut sauce over the kebabs and sprinkle with sesame seeds.

NUTRITION PER SERVE
Protein 31.5 g; Fat 65 g; Carbohydrate 25.5 g; Dietary Fibre 15 g; Cholesterol 0 mg; 3334 kJ (795 cal)

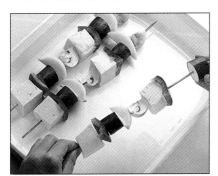

Thread alternating pieces of tofu and vegetables onto the skewers.

Cook the skewers, occasionally turning and basting them.

Simmer the peanut sauce for 10 minutes, or until just thickened.

THAI TEMPEH

Preparation time: 15 minutes +
    overnight marinating
Total cooking time: 20 minutes
Serves 4

2 stems lemon grass, finely
    chopped
2 kaffir lime leaves, shredded
2 small red chillies, seeded
    and finely chopped
3 cloves garlic, crushed
2 teaspoons sesame oil
1/2 cup (125 ml) lime juice
2 teaspoons shaved palm
    sugar
1/2 cup (125 ml) soy sauce
600 g tofu tempeh, cut into
    twelve 5 mm slices
1/4 cup (60 ml) peanut oil
1 tablespoon shaved palm
    sugar, extra
100 g snow pea sprouts or
    watercress
kaffir lime leaves, finely
    shredded, extra

1 Place the lemon grass, lime leaves, chilli, garlic, sesame oil, lime juice, sugar and soy sauce in a non-metallic bowl and mix. Add the tempeh and stir. Cover and marinate overnight in the fridge, turning occasionally.
2 Drain the tempeh, reserving the marinade. Heat half the peanut oil in a frying pan over high heat. Cook the tempeh in batches, turning once, for 5 minutes, or until crispy, adding more oil when needed. Drain on paper towels. Heat the reserved marinade with the extra palm sugar in a

saucepan until syrupy.
3 Divide one third of the tempeh among four serving plates and top with half the snow pea sprouts. Continue with the remaining ingredients to give three layers of tempeh and two layers of sprouts, finishing with the tempeh on top. Drizzle with the reserved marinade and sprinkle with extra lime leaves.

NUTRITION PER SERVE
Protein 9.5 g; Fat 20 g; Carbohydrate 7 g;
Dietary Fibre 1.5 g; Cholesterol 0 mg;
1102 kJ (262 cal)

Cook the tempeh in batches, turning once, until crispy.

Heat the reserved marinade and extra palm sugar in a saucepan until syrupy.

EGGPLANT AND MUSHROOM SKEWERS WITH TOMATO CONCASSE

Preparation time: 20 minutes +
 15 minutes marinating
Total cooking time: 25 minutes
Serves 4

  VEGAN

12 long rosemary sprigs
18 Swiss brown mushrooms
1 small eggplant, cut into
 2 cm cubes
¼ cup (60 ml) olive oil
2 tablespoons balsamic
 vinegar
2 cloves garlic, crushed
1 teaspoon sugar
olive oil, for brushing
sea salt, to sprinkle (optional)

Tomato concassé
5 tomatoes
1 tablespoon olive oil
1 small onion, finely chopped
1 clove garlic, crushed
1 tablespoon tomato paste
2 teaspoons sugar
2 teaspoons balsamic vinegar
1 tablespoon chopped fresh
 flat-leaf parsley

1 Remove the leaves from the rosemary sprigs, leaving 5 cm on the tip. Reserve 1 tablespoon of the leaves. Cut the mushrooms in half, keeping the stems intact. Place the mushrooms and eggplant in a large non-metallic bowl. Pour on the combined oil, vinegar, garlic and sugar, then season and toss. Marinate for 15 minutes.
2 Score a cross in the base of each tomato. Put in a bowl of boiling water for 30 seconds then plunge into cold water. Peel the skin away from the cross. Cut in half and scoop out the seeds with a teaspoon. Dice.
3 Heat the oil in a saucepan. Cook the onion and garlic over medium heat for 2–3 minutes, or until soft. Reduce the heat, add the tomato, tomato paste, sugar, vinegar and parsley and simmer for 10 minutes, or until the liquid has evaporated. Keep warm.
4 Thread alternating mushroom halves and eggplant cubes onto the rosemary sprigs, so there are three mushroom halves and two cubes of eggplant. Lightly oil a chargrill plate or barbecue and cook the skewers for 7–8 minutes, or until the eggplant is tender, turning occasionally. Serve with concassé and sprinkle with sea salt and the reserved rosemary.

NUTRITION PER SERVE
Protein 3 g; Fat 24 g; Carbohydrate 8.5 g; Dietary Fibre 4 g; Cholesterol 0 mg; 1100 kJ (263 cal)

Simmer the tomato sauce until it is thick and pulpy.

Thread alternating mushrooms and eggplant cubes onto the skewers.

INDEX

VEGAN RECIPES ARE INDICATED BY ITALICS.

INTERNATIONAL GLOSSARY OF INGREDIENTS

capsicum	red or green pepper	snow peas	mange tout
fresh coriander	fresh cilantro	teardrop tomato (Aus.)	yellow pear tomato (UK)
eggplant	aubergine	tomato paste (Aus.)	tomato purée, double concentrate (UK)
English spinach	spinach		
shallots (Aus.)	eschalots	zucchini	courgette

Published by Murdoch Books® , a division of Murdoch Magazines Pty Limited, GPO Box 1203 Sydney NSW 1045.

Managing Editor: Rachel Carter. **Editor:** Zoë Harpham. **Designer:** Wing Ping Tong. **Food Director:** Jody Vassallo. **Managing Food Editor:** Jane Lawson. **Food Editor:** Rebecca Clancy. **Recipe Development:** Rebecca Clancy, Judy Clarke, Michelle Earl, Lulu Grimes, Michelle Lawton, Kerrie Mullins, Kate Murdoch, Tracy Rutherford, Dimitra Stais, Jody Vassallo. **Home Economists:** Alison Adams, Michelle Lawton, Michaela Le Compte, Ben Masters, Kate Murdoch, Margot Smithyman, Michelle Thrift, Angela Tregonning. **Nutritionist:** Thérèse Abbey. **Photographers:** Roberto Jean François, Reg Morrison (steps), Lindsay Ross (cover). **Food Stylist:** Marie-Hélène Clauzon. **Food Preparation:** Ben Masters. **Nutritional text:** Jackie Reed, Jody Vassallo, Tracy Rutherford. **UK consultant:** Maggi Altham. **CEO & Publisher:** Anne Wilson.

The nutritional information provided for each recipe does not include garnishes or accompaniments, such as rice, unless they are included in specific quantities in the ingredients. The values are approximations and can be affected by biological and seasonal variations in food, the unknown composition of some manufactured foods and uncertainty in the dietary database. Nutrient data given are derived primarily from the NUTTAB95 database produced by the Australian New Zealand Food Authority. National Library of Australia Cataloguing-in-Publication Data. Delicious vegetarian food. Includes index. ISBN 0 86411 916 X . 1. Vegetarian cookery. I. Title: Family circle (Sydney, N.S.W). 641.5636.
First printed 2000. Printed by Prestige Litho, Queensland. PRINTED IN AUSTRALIA.

Copyright© Text, design, photography and illustrations Murdoch Books® 2000. All rights reserved.
No part of this publication may be reproduced, stored in a retrieval system or transmitted in any form or by any means, electronic, mechanical, photocopying, recording or otherwise without the prior written permission of the publisher. Murdoch Books® is a registered trademark of Murdoch Magazines Pty Ltd. Australian distribution to supermarkets and newsagents by Gordon and Gotch Ltd, 68 Kingsgrove Road, Belmore, NSW 2182. Distributed in NZ by Golden Press, a division of HarperCollins Publishers, 31 View Road, Glenfield, PO Box 1, Auckland 1.